Overcoming Panic a

Overcoming Panic and Panic Attacks

PHIL LANE

sheldon PRESS

First published in Great Britain by Sheldon Press in 2025
An imprint of John Murray Press

1

This book is for information or educational purposes only and is not intended to act as a substitute for medical advice or treatment. Any person with a condition requiring medical attention should consult a qualified medical practitioner or suitable therapist.

A CIP catalogue record for this title is available from the British Library

Library of Congress Control Number: 2025934246

Trade Paperback ISBN 978 1 399 81981 7
ebook ISBN 978 1 399 81982 4

Typeset by KnowledgeWorks Global Ltd.

Printed and bound in Great Britain by Clays Ltd, Elcograf S.p.A.

John Murray Press policy is to use papers that are natural, renewable and recyclable products and made from wood grown in sustainable forests. The logging and manufacturing processes are expected to conform to the environmental regulations of the country of origin.

John Murray Press
Carmelite House
50 Victoria Embankment
London EC4Y 0DZ

www.sheldonpress.co.uk

John Murray Press, part of Hodder & Stoughton Limited
An Hachette UK company

The authorised representative in the EEA is Hachette Ireland, 8 Castlecourt Centre, Dublin 15, D15 YF6A, Ireland (email: info@hbgi.ie)

Acknowledgments

I wish to thank the following individuals, all of whom played an important role in the writing of this book: first and foremost, my wife Nicole and my son Nico: thank you for all of your support and love; my late mother Carmela (Sandy) for always rooting for me; Rachel Landes at Hachette Book Group for championing this book; Matt Kirkpatrick for his editorial acuity and assistance; all of the therapists who have helped me in my personal journey to panic recovery, and all of my clients who continue to inspire me with their resilience and strength.

Contents

About the author

Phil Lane, M.S.W., L.C.S.W. is a clinical social worker and psychotherapist in private practice. He specializes in the treatment of anxiety, panic, trauma, and mood disorders. Phil is the author of the books *Understanding and Coping with Illness Anxiety* (Routledge, 2023), *The Narrative Therapy Workbook for Self-Esteem* (New Harbinger, 2025), *Overcoming Panic and Panic Attacks* (Sheldon Press, 2025), and of the ongoing blog "Am I Dying?" for *Psychology Today* magazine. He practices and writes from a humanistic and existential viewpoint, with a belief in the commonality of the human experience. Phil and his family live in Central New Jersey.

Introduction

I am not exaggerating when I say that I lived this book. My first panic attack was intense and terrifying and rocked my foundation of security. It embedded within me a fear that I was losing control, going crazy, and experiencing some sort of catastrophic medical emergency. When that first panic attack occurred, I was doing the most mundane of things—sitting at my desk at work. Nothing too intense was happening, at least nothing that warranted such a feeling of dread. But my body seemed to feel otherwise as it tightened, constricted, and elicited an emergency response. My heart fluttered and pounded uncontrollably. Lightheaded and disoriented, I left work and went to the emergency room, only to be told I was "fine." It was little reassurance, as I felt shaken and frightened by how I had felt. I did not know it at the time, but I had experienced a "textbook" panic attack.

Twenty years later, I view that first experience with panic as having had a significant role in my life. As uncomfortable and frightening as it was, that initial panic attack actually inspired me to begin therapy, to learn about the psychology of anxiety and panic and, ultimately, to enter the mental health field so that I could help others learn to manage panic. I am living proof that panic does not have to rule your life and that you can not only heal from it, but also thrive despite it.

I hope this book will educate you, comfort you, and be a part of your healing journey. The chapters of this book are designed to provide a logical progression of ideas and concepts, all toward the goal of helping you develop adaptive skills for releasing panic's grip and once again feeling safe and comfortable.

Part I
Understanding panic

The first part of this book is designed to help you understand what panic is, why it happens, and how it affects our daily lives. The understanding you will gain through these first three chapters will help you to begin feeling that panic is less of a mysterious force that you have no control over and more something that you can understand, comprehend, and control. Understanding is the first step toward healing and, as *your* grasp of panic and panic attacks strengthens, panic's grasp on you loosens.

1

Panic defined

This chapter will help you understand what panic is and how it can feel when it occurs. While this chapter will share some basic information on brain function and other physical systems, you do not need to have a deep scientific understanding of these concepts; the idea is to understand in a basic sense how your brain and body respond to panic.

Anxiety versus panic

Anxiety and panic, while similar to one another, are not one and the same though they are often spoken about interchangeably. Understanding the difference between the two is crucial before you can fully understand panic and panic attacks. In simple terms, **anxiety** is defined by prolonged feelings of worry that vary in intensity, whereas **panic** is acute and intense, often lasting only a few minutes, but an extremely uncomfortable and frightening few minutes.

Anxiety often precedes panic and can sometimes cause panic to occur, particularly when it becomes overwhelming and persistent. Anxiety is typically brought on by a specific, identifiable activating event, or trigger, while panic can occur unexpectedly. For example, you may experience anxiety ahead of an important work or school presentation, whereas panic may not necessarily be connected to a specific event or situation. The chart below outlines what you may commonly experience when you are anxious versus what you may experience when you are panicked.

Anxiety	Panic
Uncomfortable, but not necessarily intense, physical symptoms.	Intense physical symptoms that cause significant distress.
Can last an extended period of time, even days or weeks.	Typically short in duration, usually lasting a few minutes.
Often logically connected to a specific event or situation.	Often not easily connected to a single, identifiable event or situation.
Generalized feelings of uneasiness and discomfort.	Specific physical symptoms and sensations of severe discomfort.
"Free-floating" feelings of worry that can vary and change in intensity.	Acute feelings of dread that are consistently intense.

These distinctions between anxiety and panic are helpful in not confusing the two and in understanding why panic experiences can be so much greater in intensity and can feel more difficult to manage.

Panic attacks defined

Specific diagnostic criteria describes what commonly occurs during experiences of panic. The information that follows from the American Psychiatric Association's *Diagnostic and Statistical Manual of Mental Disorders* (Fifth Edition Text Revision) is intended not to help you self-diagnose but rather to conceptualize and understand how panic disorder is defined. Please note that only a credentialed mental health professional can make an accurate clinical diagnosis.

Diagnostic Criteria of Panic Disorder (F41.0)

A. Recurrent unexpected panic attacks. A panic attack is an abrupt surge of intense fear or intense discomfort that reaches a peak within minutes, and during which time four (or more) of the following symptoms occur:

Note: The abrupt surge can occur from a calm state or an anxious state.

1 Palpitations, pounding heart, or accelerated heart rate.
2 Sweating.
3 Trembling or shaking.
4 Sensations of shortness of breath or smothering.
5 Feelings of choking.
6 Chest pain or discomfort.
7 Nausea or abdominal distress.
8 Feeling dizzy, unsteady, light-headed, or faint.
9 Chills or heat sensations.
10 Paresthesias (numbness or tingling sensations).
11 Derealization (feelings of unreality) or depersonalization (being detached from oneself).
12 Fear of losing control or "going crazy."
13 Fear of dying.

Note: Culture-specific symptoms (e.g., tinnitus, neck soreness, headache, uncontrollable screaming or crying) may be seen. Such symptoms should not count as one of the four required symptoms.

B. At least one of the attacks has been followed by 1 month (or more) of both of the following:

1 Persistent concern or worry about additional panic attacks or their consequences (e.g., losing control, having a heart attack, "going crazy").
2 A significant maladaptive change in behavior related to the attacks (e.g., behaviors designed to avoid having panic attacks, such as avoidance of exercise or unfamiliar situations).

C. The disturbance is not attributable to the physiological effects of a substance (e.g., a drug of abuse, medication) or another medical condition (e.g., hyperthyroidism, cardiopulmonary disorders).

D. The disturbance is not better explained by another mental disorder (e.g., the panic attacks do not occur only in response to feared social situations, as in social anxiety disorder; in response to circumscribed phobic objects or situations, as in specific phobia; in response to obsessions, as in obsessive-compulsive disorder; in response to reminders of traumatic events, as in posttraumatic stress disorder; or in response to separation from attachment figures, as in separation anxiety disorder).[1]

Panic attacks can take their own form for different individuals. You may experience a few or many of the symptoms described above, but what you experience may be different from what another individual experiences when they have a panic attack. It is helpful to understand what symptoms commonly occur during panic and panic attacks. Below, you will find further explanations of each of the commonly experienced criteria of panic attacks:

Palpitations

An accelerated heart rate is common during a panic attack. When this happens, you may feel like your heart is fluttering, pounding, or beating too fast.

Sweating

Sweating is how your body attempts to soothe itself and to cool down its temperature. So, though uncomfortable, sweating is actually your body's way of trying to calm itself. It stands to reason, then, that, while in a panic state, you may experience perspiration more than you would in a calmer state.

Trembling or shaking

In a state of overwhelm, your body responds much like an overheated car: it ceases to run smoothly and, instead, feels unsteady, wobbly, and shaky. Your body may feel unsteady, and you may experience sensations of shakiness when you are panicked.

Shortness of breath

During a panic attack, it is common to feel that you are unable to catch your breath. Your respiratory system kicks into overdrive and becomes stressed, and therefore your breathing can feel labored.

Feelings of choking

Think of panic as a tightening of your body. As muscles, airways, and joints become tight, they naturally feel constricted. In this state, it can feel difficult to swallow, which can create the sensation that you are choking.

Chest pain

Panic is commonly felt in the chest and heart. Panic sensations can present as pain and tightness in the chest, and/or extreme general discomfort in your chest cavity and heart area.

Nausea or abdominal distress

The gastrointestinal system is one of the body's most intense responders to panic. You may experience:

- nausea
- stomach pain
- diarrhea
- vomiting.

Dizziness

Think about your body as being "off-kilter" when it is panicked. In these times, you tend to lose your sense of grounding, and therefore feel shaky, dizzy, and lightheaded.

Chills or heat sensation

Your body's systems of regulation are impacted by panic. In an overwhelmed state, your body may struggle to regulate its temperature, resulting in chills or feelings of being overheated.

Derealization or depersonalization

Intense panic attacks can bring about a feeling of unreality, in which you feel "out of touch" with what is happening. Similarly, you may feel as if you are having an out-of-body experience. These feelings are due to the intensity of your body's fear response.

Fear of losing control

In the throes of a panic attack, it can be difficult to make sense of what is happening. This can bring on feelings that you are spiraling out of control and that you do not have a firm grip on yourself or on the situation.

Fear of dying

Because many of the symptoms described above mimic more serious medical problems, the anxious conclusion that is often drawn during a panic attack is that you are dying. While it is actually not possible to die from a panic attack, it can feel as though your life is in peril.

Panic attacks versus anxiety attacks

We should note a necessary distinction: a panic attack and an anxiety attack are not interchangeable. The main differences are intensity and duration. A panic attack is generally very intense and swift whereas an anxiety attack is more drawn out and less intense, though similarly uncomfortable. Anxiety attacks can persist at a moderate level of intensity for as long as a few days while a panic attack will persist for only a few minutes at its peak level of intensity.

Panic attack subtypes

Above, you learned about the general criteria for a panic attack. While panic attacks may produce many of these symptoms, recent psychological literature identifies four distinct subtypes of a panic attack that are commonly reported:[2]

- Cardiac
- Respiratory
- Gastrointestinal
- Vestibular.

In each, the panic symptoms tend to be localized to specific regions of the body, rather than experienced across the systems. Your unique presentation of panic may fall into one of these subtypes, or it may be more generalized. Understanding how your panic presents itself is helpful in beginning to recognize panic's onset and how and where it occurs for you. The diagram below illustrates the common places where panic subtypes occur.

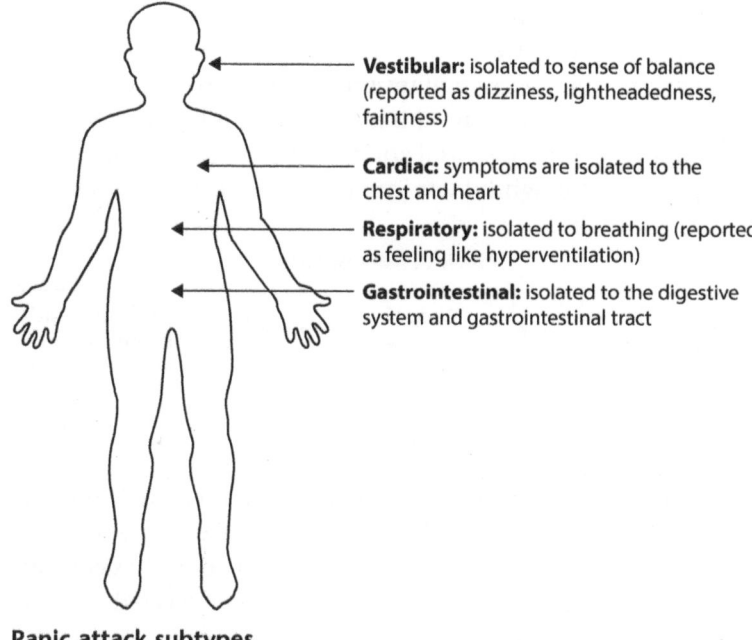

Vestibular: isolated to sense of balance (reported as dizziness, lightheadedness, faintness)

Cardiac: symptoms are isolated to the chest and heart

Respiratory: isolated to breathing (reported as feeling like hyperventilation)

Gastrointestinal: isolated to the digestive system and gastrointestinal tract

Panic attack subtypes

A primitive response

We can base our understanding of panic on a very simple fact: panic is a **primitive response**. Ironically, this runs contrary to a basic truth about our lives: we are sophisticated, highly intelligent, and complex. Our lives contain many layers and situations and are rich and nuanced. But panic is an overly simplistic and animalistic reaction to conditions. But think about it this way: in primitive times, early humans were in constant, tangible danger from wild carnivores and harsh environmental conditions, were susceptibility to physical injury, and needed to hunt prey by moving dangerously close to other predators.[3] Given these persistent and obvious threats, it was necessary for humans to be perpetually on guard, cautious, and ready to flee or fight. In our more sophisticated times, however, this type of emergency response is often unnecessary and may be viewed as an overreaction.

But our brains do not always know the difference between a situation that is truly dangerous and one that is less threatening. As complex and sophisticated as they are, our brains sometimes struggle to differentiate between safety and danger in modern society. At some level, we still possess a **mammalian brain**, which responds to stimuli in an animalistic way. This is what panic is like: it can present as an automatic, primitive, and animalistic response that lacks deep investigation or thoughtfulness into what is *really* happening.

Primitive fear response

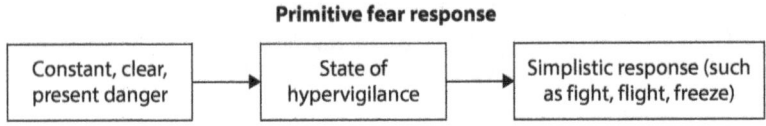

Triggers

Something—real or imagined—has to happen for our panic response to kick in. We refer to these activating events, situations, and experiences as **triggers**, which essentially "switch on" our physical panic response. As a simple example, consider an unexpected thunderclap. You are sitting calmly and quietly when, suddenly, an incredibly loud burst of thunder echoes through your house. Your body responds to this unexpected stimulus by startling, trembling, and feeling instantaneously unsafe. Your heart rate quickens, you begin to sweat, and you feel uncomfortable.

Triggers activate our panic response in the same way. Of course, the triggers we may experience are often more complex than a loud sound: they may be related to our emotions and, thus, far more difficult to pinpoint.

Taking this simple concept a step further, we might view triggers this way:

Triggers

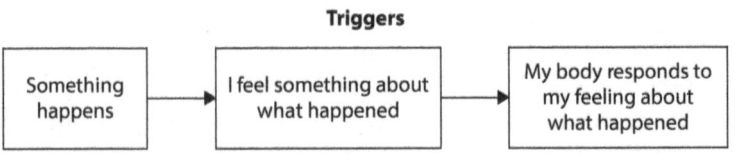

In Chapter 2, we will further explore specific triggers and how they can impact panic responses. Understanding and beginning to identify your triggers can help you learn to reduce the impact of panic on your life.

Perceived danger versus tangible danger

The dangers we face in our modern lives are often *perceived* rather than *tangible*. For example, while we are no longer at risk of attack by saber-toothed tigers or cave bears, we may feel at risk of:

- humiliation
- failure
- judgement by others
- illness
- aging

... and a host of other common discomforts.

Notice that many of the things we feel unsafe about in our modern lives tend to be potentialities or "what ifs" rather than clear and present dangers such as deadly predators. The key component to understand is that our bodies cannot always tell the difference between a *perceived* danger and a *tangible* danger. The primitive fear response still exists within us and is easily triggered in the same way it was for our early hominid ancestors.

Our bodies, as sophisticated as they are, struggle at times to differentiate between something that *might* happen and something that *is* happening. In these moments, they elicit an emergency response by releasing **cortisol**, the body's naturally occurring stress hormone. This, in turn, activates panic signals which present as accelerated heart rate, perspiration, quickened respiration, and other commonly experienced physical responses.

Fight, flight, and freeze

You might be wondering "But why?" Why do I feel these uncomfortable and distressing feelings? Using the idea of early hominids as a guide, view your fear responses as being essentially categorized by **fighting, fleeing, or freezing**. In simple terms, there were occasions when it was best to fight, best to run, and best to stay put. For example, a cave dweller might shelter in place (freeze) during extreme weather, run (flee) from a dangerous predator, or defend themselves (fight) against a less dangerous creature.

We elicit these same three fear responses in our modern lives: at times, we unconsciously choose any of them to respond to stimulus. For instance, we might react angrily (fight), leave a situation that feels overwhelming (flee), or become avoidant (freeze). In terms of panic, these responses are never well thought out; rather, they are automatic reactions to what we perceive as dangerous situations. This categorization of responses, while simplistic, creates a basic understanding of what the body is doing when it responds with panic: it is either fighting, fleeing, or freezing.

FIGHT	FLIGHT	FREEZE
Go toward feared stimulus	Avoid feared stimulus	Become paralyzed by feared stimulus

Understanding your nervous system

So, who is in charge of these responses? What directs the body to respond in the ways described above? In basic terms, we can break down the larger **autonomic nervous system**, which controls involuntary processes such as heart rate, respiration, and digestion into two distinct parts: the **sympathetic nervous system**, which controls the fight-or-fight, flight, or freeze response and the **parasympathetic nervous system**, which carries the signals that allow the body to relax.

In times of stress or intense stimulus, the sympathetic nervous system becomes overactive and overrides the parasympathetic nervous system, causing the body to transmit panic signals and experience frightening symptoms, such as those described in the diagnostic criteria at the beginning of this chapter.[4] Ironically, the very system that is intended to keep us safe actually ends up frightening us when it becomes overactive. This simple understanding of the two systems and what they do can help you to pay attention to times when a system becomes flooded and how this causes your body to respond.

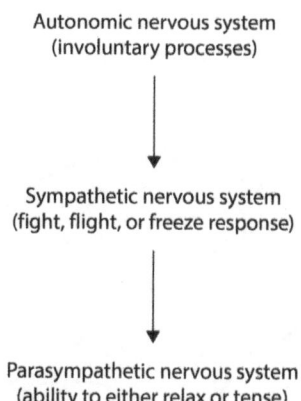

Autonomic nervous system
(involuntary processes)

Sympathetic nervous system
(fight, flight, or freeze response)

Parasympathetic nervous system
(ability to either relax or tense)

Panic attacks and the brain

Two key parts of the brain are responsible for how your nervous systems become activated or, in the case of panic, overactivated. Your brain is the central command center for everything that happens in your body. It receives external stimuli and messages and responds by sending instructions down the spinal column and through the body. The body receives these instructions and responds accordingly. If, for example, the instructions say, "hunker down," the body responds by freezing, constricting, and tightening up.

Your **prefrontal cortex (PFC)** is sort of like the doorway to your brain: it receives information and—most of the time—analyzes it rationally and logically. It decides how to proceed with the information and what action, if any, needs to be taken based on the information. Panic, however, can disrupt the PFC's ability to analyze information rationally and, instead, cause it to categorize an innocuous stimulus as dangerous.[5]

When this happens, the PFC alerts the **amygdala**, the part of the brain that holds our fear response, and directs the body to release physical survival responses such as increased respiration, accelerated heart rate, perspiration, and any of the other common symptoms described earlier. In his book *The Body Keeps the Score*, psychiatrist Bessel van der Kolk likens the amygdala to a smoke detector and explains that its "central function ... is to identify whether incoming input is relevant for our survival. It does so quickly and automatically."[6] Once the amygdala is activated, the body's fear response kicks into overdrive and we experience those emergency physical symptoms.

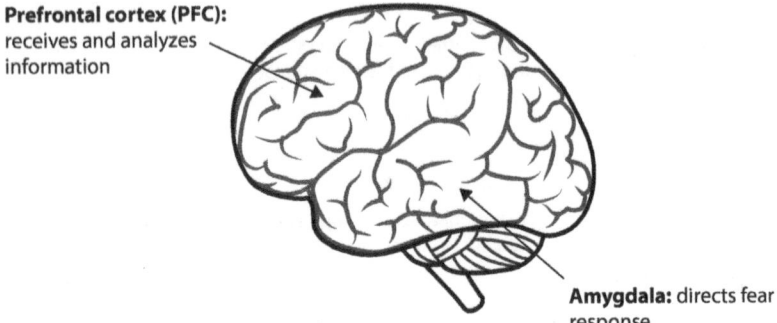

Prefrontal cortex (PFC): receives and analyzes information

Amygdala: directs fear response

Crossed signals

The systems within the body described above (the nervous systems, prefrontal cortex, and amygdala) usually work in tandem with one another and function effectively and properly. When we panic, however, our internal systems' signals get crossed, and the body becomes confused as to how to respond. It pumps out too much of this, too little of that. Intense bodily chaos results, and you feel the symptoms and sensations described earlier. When the body is confused, it stands to reason that the mind will be confused as well. In these situations, the mind tells us things that are untrue like "I'm having a heart attack" or "I'm dying." In moments of panic, these anxious conclusions can feel like absolute truths and it can be difficult to rationally challenge them. Many individuals who experience panic attacks (myself included) will go to the emergency room, misinterpreting the panic symptoms as signs of a true medical emergency.

Differentiating between a panic attack and a medical emergency

Many panic symptoms, particularly the subtypes described above, can imitate serious medical conditions and cause us to worry that we are having a medical emergency. **Somatic mimics** such as chest pain that is interpreted as a heart attack or a headache that is interpreted as an aneurysm can cause significant distress. Understanding how panic sensations can mimic more emergent symptoms is vital in learning to differentiate between the two, and not cause yourself to assume you are experiencing a catastrophic health issue. Many commonly misinterpreted physical symptoms are better explained as arising as the result of panic. The chart below shows five commonly misinterpreted physical symptoms often brought on by panic.

Panic attack symptom	Common misinterpretation
Chest pain/palpitations	Heart attack/cardiac emergency
Gastrointestinal discomfort	Stomach cancer/appendicitis
Dizziness	Seizure/loss of consciousness
Shortness of breath	Choking/heart attack
Depersonalization	Psychiatric emergency (psychotic break, etc.)

Please note that this is not to suggest that you shouldn't seek emergency medical care when required, but rather to help you understand that at times, panic-related symptoms are misinterpreted as requiring such care. You should stay on top of your physical health by attending yearly checkups and following provider guidance so you can rule out symptoms that are attributable to panic rather than to other medical issues.

Aaron

Twenty-seven-year-old Aaron, an emergency medical technician who commonly worked a 60-hour workweek, had been feeling dizzy for a few days. While he could still go to work and carry out his daily routine, he just felt, as he described it, "off." After three days of feeling this way, Aaron decided to visit the emergency room. Since the onset of the symptoms, he had become more and more worried and was too anxious to wait for an appointment with his primary care doctor. When asked at intake what had brought him into the hospital, he struggled to pinpoint or describe his symptoms, responding "I feel off. I've been kind of dizzy and just feeling like something is wrong." Aaron was admitted and underwent a variety of tests. After six hours in the hospital, he was discharged with the information that nothing was out of order and he appeared to be a healthy young man.

Aaron felt both relived and dissatisfied with this information. On the one hand, he was glad to hear that nothing terrible had been found, but, on the other hand, he lacked an answer as to why he had been feeling "off." Without a solid answer, Aaron felt worried that his feelings of discomfort would only continue. It is often only by accepting the impact of anxiety, worry, stress, and other life circumstances that a person learns to let go of fixating on the "why" of panic. As there is no blood test, x-ray, or scan that can detect anxiety, individuals are often left having to recognize this connection for themselves. For Aaron, a better understanding of his larger life circumstances was helpful in uncovering what may have contributed to his physical discomfort and symptoms.

Viewing the larger life circumstances

Aaron worked a hectic schedule at a stressful job, consumed a great deal of caffeine in order to stay alert, and often felt exhausted by his work, which was often fast-paced and emotionally taxing. While he tried his best to relax when he was able, he still frequently felt tired and overwhelmed by his job. After a long shift, he would often feel "keyed up" and find it difficult to unwind from the day. Understanding the impact of Aaron's current life circumstances is helpful to recognize why he may be susceptible to symptoms related to panic.

Take a few moments to ask yourself the questions below in order to help you find areas where your life circumstances may be impacting the physical symptoms you experience.

- How has my sleep been?
- Do I consistently stay hydrated?
- Do I maintain a healthy diet?
- Do I get adequate physical exercise and movement?
- Do I use substances such as alcohol and marijuana in moderation?
- Do I have a healthy work–life balance?

- What is my caffeine/simulant consumption like?
- Do I have adequate time for myself and for self-care activities?
- What is my level of overwhelm and burnout?
- Am I consistently stressed or worried?

What is my emotional state? Am I going through any difficult situations in my life?

These are questions you can always keep in your mind to help you recognize when what is happening in your life may be influencing feelings and symptoms of panic. Were Aaron to pay more attention to his extenuating life circumstances, he might realize that such a fast-paced and stressful work life is likely a direct contributor to his panic. It might help Aaron to reassess his relationship with his job and find healthy ways care for himself and reduce his stress.

The importance of understanding

You might be wondering "Do I really need to know all this technical stuff about the nervous system and the brain? This isn't a science class." But think of it this way: when we understand something, it loses its mystique, and we gain a sense of control over what had previously been hard to fathom.

In my own experience, once I began to understand what panic was, how it worked, and how it affected me uniquely, I started to feel it had less power over my life. It went from being something that was wholly beyond my control to something I could comprehend and learn to manage.

Hopefully this chapter has provided you with a basic comprehension of what panic is and why it occurs. It is through this understanding and knowledge that you can begin to heal.

Exercises and activities

With all you have learned in this chapter in mind, complete the exercises and activities below as a way to begin building a coping "toolbox" for navigating feelings of panic.

Psychoeducation checklist

The idea of understanding the psychology that underlies what we experience in our lives, or "psychoeducation," is helpful in cultivating a feeling of power over our challenges. Below, having read this chapter, place a checkmark beside each statement that you feel is true:

☐ I feel that I have a basic understanding of how the brain and the nervous system impact anxiety and panic.

☐ I feel that I understand the difference between anxiety and panic.

☐ The symptoms described in this chapter make sense and help me feel that what I experience when I am panicked is not uncommon.

☐ I understand how panic can be described as a "primitive response."

☐ I understand how panic symptoms can mimic more serious medical conditions and problems.

When we experience panic, things feel as though they are moving at lightning speed. Slow yourself down with grounding techniques during these moments. These types of techniques allow you to return to a state of equilibrium.

3-3-3 strategy for grounding

The 3-3-3 strategy works by identifying and paying mindful attention to three objects, three sounds, and three body parts. Paying attention allows us to step out of our panic mindset and into a calmer sphere. Below are spaces for you to utilize this strategy in moments when you are feeling overwhelmed and flooded:

Three objects I can identify:

_____

_____

_____

Three sounds I can hear:

_____

_____

_____

Three body parts I can move:

_____

_____

_____

By slowing down and focusing your attention using this 3-3-3 strategy, you should hopefully experience a sense of grounding and calm. You can utilize this strategy any time you are feeling panicky.

Key terms

Anxiety: Prolonged feelings of worry that are typically less intense than panic feelings.

Panic: Acute and intense feelings of dread that typically manifest with frightening physical symptoms.

Cardiac subtype: Panic symptoms that are localized to the chest and heart area.

Respiratory subtype: Panic symptoms that are localized to the respiratory system.

Gastrointestinal subtype: Panic symptoms that are localized to the gastrointestinal tract.

Vestibular subtype: Panic symptoms that are localized to the body's sense of balance and equilibrium.

Somatic mimic: Panic symptoms that imitate more serious medical conditions.

Mammalian brain: The primitive brain and how it responds to stimulus, typically resulting in a "fight, flight, or freeze" response.

Triggers: Events, situations, or stimuli that "activate" our panic response.

Fight, flight, and freeze: The three basic fear responses, which take the form of going toward the feared stimulus (fight), running from the stimulus (flight), or becoming paralyzed by the stimulus (freeze).

Prefrontal cortex: The part of the brain that receives information and, when in a calm state, rationally and logically analyzes it to determine how to respond.

Amygdala: The "smoke detector" of the brain, which determines when a stimulus is dangerous and requires an emergency response.

Autonomic nervous system: The system that controls involuntary processes such as heart rate, respiration, and digestion.

Sympathetic nervous system: The system that controls the body's fight, flight, or freeze response.

Parasympathetic nervous system: The system that carries the signals which allow the body to rest and relax.

2

Why panic happens

Now that you understand *how* panic attacks happen, you are probably wondering *why* they happen. While there are a variety of answers to this question, we will explore some of the common reasons in this chapter.

A primitive response in a sophisticated world

In the previous chapter, we described panic as a primitive response. Let's discuss the world we live in and how, at times, it can be "fertile ground" for anxiety and panic responses. Life in the twenty-first century is complicated and often stressful. You need only scroll through news alerts on your phone to find proof of this. While what we encounter today is different than what our early hominid ancestors dealt with, it can often provoke the same type of primitive response. The difference lies in *what* we encounter: no longer are these frightening stimuli things like wild predators; rather they are typically situations based in the following:

- overstimulating environments
- trauma
- chronic stress
- significant life changes
- repressed or suppressed emotions
- specific phobias
- a family history of panic disorder.

This chapter will explore each of these possible activators of panic and provide accompanying examples to help you understand how each underlying cause can influence panic and panic attacks.

Overstimulating environments

Our lives tend to be busy, chaotic, and overwhelming at times. A constant sense of movement and stimulation can be an activator of our panic response. Below, you will read about Louise, whose experience while driving on a busy highway provoked a panic response.

Louise

Louise, a 63-year-old sales representative, was driving to an offsite work location one morning. It was a sunny day with clear weather and blue skies. She had been to this site numerous times before and knew the route without needing to rely on GPS. Louise's route took her along a very busy stretch of highway which, at one point, expanded to five lanes of traffic. On this part of the roadway, there were numerous entrance and exit ramps and traffic merging swiftly into the primary lanes of travel.

As Louise guided her car around a curvy portion of the highway, she felt suddenly dizzy and a feeling of unreality overcame her. She noticed her heart pounding and her breath becoming labored. A frightening conclusion flashed across her mind: "I am having a heart attack and am going to crash my car." Louise, unsure that she could safely continue driving, pulled the car safely to the side of the highway and called her daughter to come and pick her up. When her daughter came, she insisted that Louise go to the emergency room, as neither of them was able to identify what had happened as a panic attack.

At the hospital, Louise underwent a variety of tests and scans, only to reveal that nothing signaling a health problem—let alone a heart attack—had been discovered.

Louise's panic response

Unsure of what to make of what had happened and with no clear answer, Louise decided that the best option was to stop driving on highways altogether. The next time her job required her to visit the offsite location, Louise found a route that completely avoided highway travel. Though this circuitous route added nearly an hour to her trip, Louise felt safer knowing that she would not be traveling on the highway where she had experienced the frightening situation. From that point on, Louise would go to great lengths to map out routes to places that did not require her to travel by highway.

Our flight response is a response of avoidance. To guard ourselves from frightening stimulus, we remove ourselves from anything even vaguely similar to the perceived dangerous stimulus. Louise's response of completely avoiding highways, while somewhat understandable based on her experience, is also **maladaptive** because it prevents her from adapting to a situation in a healthy or creative way. In our modern lives, fight, flight, and freeze responses are often maladaptive because they cause us to take an extreme response to a frightening situation rather than a more measured and rational approach. When we respond maladaptively, we often fail to recognize that more adaptive means are available to us.

A more **adaptive** response might be for Louise to seek psychotherapy or other support for help with her highway-related fears, or to try to travel by highway again without assuming that what happened before will occur again. She might also implement other more adaptive behaviors, such as asking her daughter to come along with her until she feels safe traveling alone again.

How overstimulating environments can cause panic:

• Increased release of stress hormones can occur when we are overstimulated.
• We may incorrectly assume that "busy" equates to "unsafe or dangerous," resulting in the body releasing too much cortisol and causing us to feel panicky.

Have you ever experienced panic in response to an overstimulating environment? If so, where? What were the circumstances? Write down what happened during your experience and the feelings and symptoms you experienced. What are the adaptive measures you might consider to help you overcome this?

_____

_____

_____

_____

_____

Trauma

We now understand traumatic events to encompass much more than soldiers' experience in combat. We can be traumatized by any number of events and situations, from the seemingly "everyday," such as inconsistent parenting or toxic supervisors, to the more "severe," such as violence or physical abuse. When we experience trauma, we often feel that our sense of safety has been shattered and we will do anything to regain a feeling of security. Panic is often born of these traumatic experiences. In her book *Trauma and Recovery*, Judith Lewis Herman sums it up this way: "After a traumatic experience, the human system of self-preservation seems to go onto permanent alert, as if the danger might return at any moment."[1]

Jennifer
14-year-old Jennifer was sitting in the school cafeteria eating lunch when a "shelter-in-place" was announced over the loudspeaker. The school principal who was making the announcement stressed that this was "not a drill." Immediately, Jennifer's mind flooded with images of school shooters rampaging the school building. Moments later, five police officers rushed into the cafeteria and arrested two students who had brought fake guns into the building.

Jennifer's panic response
Although no actual weapons were involved and the student body wasn't in true danger, the incident and Jennifer's firsthand exposure to it had understandably shaken her and left an imprint on her mind. She began to experience constant nightmares which would vividly replay the events of that day. As is common in traumatic experiences, Jennifer felt she was no longer safe. She dreaded going to the cafeteria and would often eat her lunch in the school nurse's office. The nurse, who was patient, understanding, and compassionate of Jennifer's experience, helped her to feel it would be safe to begin eating in the cafeteria again. Jennifer did so slowly, at first just a day or two a week and, eventually, most days.

Months later, when an assembly was to be held in the cafeteria, Jennifer experienced an acute panic attack while walking to the assembly, in which she felt she could not breathe and might faint.

A **restoration of safety** is necessary for individuals who have experienced trauma. Jennifer, in electing to eat her lunch in the safety of the nurse's office, was attempting to find a safe place that would not bring back memories of the traumatic event in the cafeteria. The nurse assured Jennifer that she could always come to eat in her office if she so chose. Often, safety is restored through empathy and an understanding of why an individual feels afraid.

Later, Jennifer had another panic attack when walking to the cafeteria because this type of re-exposure to the location where a traumatic event occurred often triggers the body's panic response. The brain and the body both have strong memories: Jennifer's brain remembered the incident, and her body responded to the memory by eliciting its panic response.

How trauma can cause panic:

- Traumatic events instill a continued sense of danger.
- The body responds to a similar stimulus with panic sensations.
- Trauma causes individuals to take maladaptive and avoidant measures to ensure safety.

Have you experienced any traumatic events that you feel have contributed to your panic response? If so, what did you experience? How did it affect you? What might help you to restore your sense of safety? *As you answer this question, please keep in mind that the purpose of this exercise is to draw a connection between your experiences and panic, not to cause you any additional emotional discomfort. If you feel overwhelmed by this question, please feel free to skip it.*

_____

_____

_____

_____

_____

Vicarious trauma

The type of trauma in Jennifer's case was of a direct nature, in that she experienced a traumatic event in a very personal way. **Vicarious trauma**, on the other hand, does not happen to us directly but affects us in a profound way as we witness or are exposed to someone else's trauma. This is extremely common among people who work in professions like emergency medicine and triage as well as individuals who are constantly exposed to difficult situations. It can, however, affect people of all occupations and walks of life. For instance, a person who overexposes themselves to media stories of violence may experience vicarious trauma. This type of trauma can result from many different stimuli. Persistent exposure to frightening or overwhelming situations can activate our panic response.

Max

Max had worked for the past ten years as a home health aide, supporting and caring for patients who were often severely or terminally ill and who required constant care. He would often develop personal relationships with his patients and had a knack for connecting with them and building a supportive rapport. Because he worked with a geriatric population, the people he cared for would often die while in his care. While this was the nature of his work, Max was often deeply affected when one of his patients passed away, and he would feel as though he had lost a member of his own family. Over time, as Max witnessed more of his patients passing away, it began to take a toll on him.

Max's panic response

While neither Max nor an actual member of his family was ill, the impact of constantly being around sick and dying people caused him to experience panic. At the end of his shift, Max would often feel exhausted, both emotionally and physically. One evening as he was driving home after a ten-hour shift with a terminally ill cancer patient, Max began to feel lightheaded and overheated. He was not sure what was happening, and he felt frightened by the physical symptoms he was experiencing.

How vicarious trauma can cause panic:

- Continued witnessing of and exposure to difficult and traumatic events and situations can provoke feelings of panic.
- Accumulation of emotionally difficult experiences can cause bodily responses of overwhelm and panic.

Have you been exposed to any vicarious traumas in your life? If so, what are they and how might they contribute to feelings of panic? What parallels can you draw between traumas you have witnessed and your own panic response?

_____

_____

_____

_____

_____

Chronic or undiagnosable pain

Anything that does not have a clear answer can cause us to feel frustrated and unsafe. Chronic pain is not always clearly definable and can therefore leave us feeling we are persistently at risk. Symptoms that cannot be easily explained or defined can create opportunities for us to jump to catastrophic conclusions. When we do this, our panic response becomes activated and we are often flooded and overwhelmed.

Anthony
Fifty-six-year-old Anthony had spent three decades as a construction worker. Over time, the nature of his work began to take a toll on his body. He experienced constant aches and pains. Though he had visited numerous doctors, no one was able to definitively diagnose his physical pain.

Anthony's panic response

At times when he experienced pain in his back or groin, Anthony's mind jumped to the conclusion that it signaled a serious medical condition such as cancer. In these moments, he experienced panic symptoms such as quickened heartbeat and labored breathing. He visited doctor after doctor, sought out specialists, and tirelessly researched his symptoms in his search for an answer to his pain.

Anthony's response to his discomfort was often one of care-seeking. This type of behavior, though intended to find reassurance and safety, can actually worsen panic feelings, as the continued lack of definitive answers leads to increased feelings of uncertainty.

Learning to let go of the need for an exact answer can help us to pivot toward management rather than investigation. For Anthony, recognizing that the pain he experienced, while uncomfortable, was not a signal of a deeper or catastrophic medical issue, helped him to avoid reaching a state of panic in response to his physical symptoms and, instead, to focus on how to manage them.

How chronic pain can cause panic:

- Anxious assumptions and conclusions can be drawn from physical pain that cannot be clearly diagnosed and can escalate to panic.
- Benign but uncomfortable physical symptoms can be misinterpreted as signifying a medical condition that requires emergency treatment.

Are there any ways in which chronic pain may be influencing your panic response? If so, how might you, as Anthony did, turn your attention away from anxious conclusions or care-seeking and toward management of symptoms?

_____

_____

_____

_____

Significant life changes

Life changes and transitions can bring with them feelings of overwhelm, uncertainty, and discomfort. It is helpful to recognize that it is not uncommon to experience heightened emotions when you are in the midst of a significant life change. In the introduction, I shared a little bit about my own experiences with panic. In the following case example of myself, I will share more to help you understand how life changes can influence panic.

Phil (author)
At the time I began to experience persistent panic attacks, I had recently moved to a different area of my home state. It was my first time purchasing a home, which had been a stressful and overwhelming process. I worried constantly about finances and the stress of taking on a mortgage as a single person was immense. The house was located at a higher elevation than I had ever lived at before, and the weather was often severe, as the wind would whip off the shores of the state's largest lake, whose eastern end lay at the bottom of the street. I moved into the house in the dead of winter, and it was frequently snowy, icy, cold, and windy. I was about an hour's drive from my family and friends, and the entire area was brand new to me.

Phil's panic response
This life change coincided with the onset of my panic attacks. Perhaps it was the combination of financial worry, isolation, and adjusting to a new location; whatever the exact recipe, the result was a persistent feeling of dread and of something "bad" waiting to happen. My panic symptoms would come seemingly without warning. One minute, I would feel fine or be on my way to work, and the next, I would feel dizzy, my heart would palpitate, and I would tremble uncontrollably, convinced of a serious medical emergency unfolding. It wasn't until later that I connected these symptoms and sensations with the life change I had undergone.

Unlike Louise, who became completely avoidant in response to her experience with panic, my response took a mixed presentation: at times, I would avoid certain situations while, at other times, I would force myself toward situations, convinced I just needed to push myself into them. Neither extreme ended up being all that helpful.

Often, what we really need is to understand where our panic is coming from, which can inform us of the best way to cope with it. What helped me more than anything was understanding panic. I was lucky to connect with a wonderful psychologist who gently explained panic and anxiety to me and helped me to understand that the life changes I was going through were likely at the root of my panic attacks. Gradually, I was able to step back into my life and the panic attacks dwindled.

How significant life changes can cause panic:

- Changes to situations that have become expected and comfortable can provoke feelings of uncertainty and panic symptoms.
- New and different situations can be misinterpreted as dangerous situations, resulting in increased feelings of anxiety and panic.

My response to the life change of moving, taking on a mortgage, and living in a new area is one of the commonly experienced transitions that people go through. Here are some others that may influence how we respond emotionally:

Commonly experienced life changes:[2]

- Death of a spouse or close family member
- Major personal injury or illness
- Divorce or marital separation
- Marriage or pregnancy
- Firing or retirement from work
- Major change in the health of a loved one
- Major change in financial state
- Changing to a different line of work
- Taking on or foreclosing on a mortgage or loan
- Incarceration in jail or other institution
- Major change in living condition

- Major changes in working hours or conditions
- Changes in residence
- Changing to a new school

List other life changes and transitions you may be experiencing here:

_____

_____

_____

How might any life changes you are going through impact the panic that you experience? What connections can you draw between life situations and your panic response?

_____

_____

_____

_____

_____

Repressed or suppressed emotions

When we hold things in, they tend to find a way out. This simple concept speaks to panic's ability to find a way to manifest itself despite our better intentions to keep it buried. **Repression** (unconscious) and **suppression** (conscious) of difficult feelings and emotions are defense mechanisms which are intended to keep us safe but which, ironically, can lead us to feeling unsafe and panicked.

Charles

Charles had a childhood marked by parents who argued constantly. At times, either his mother or father would storm angrily out of the house, leaving Charles to wonder whether they were leaving for good. Though his parents always returned eventually and though these incidents were now decades in the past, Charles never forgot them and, while he tried to bury them deep down into his subconscious, their impact remained strong and they would manifest themselves through a fear of abandonment in Charles's current life.

Charles's panic response

Now in his early forties, Charles often ran into the same problem in his dating life: he would grow close to a potential partner but feel wracked with worry that the other person was not really invested and might leave at any moment. If too long a period of time went by between communications, Charles's body would produce panic signals: he would perspire, feel the urge to urinate frequently, and feel fidgety and uneasy, finding it difficult to settle himself down. During these occasions, Charles would try to obtain constant reassurance from his partner, often reaching out again and again to ensure that he was not being abandoned.

Charles's repressed memories of this parents' relationship directly influenced his ability to feel secure in his own relationships. Though he tried to protect himself by not thinking about his parents' marriage and how it had made him feel as a young child, this repression and suppression found its way out in his feelings of insecurity in his love life, which often manifested through panic symptoms. This is the way that these types of pushed-down feelings can manifest as panic and panic attacks. It would be helpful for Charles to confront these repressed feelings in a healthy way and in a safe environment such as a therapy session, so that they can be processed and moved on from.

How suppressed or repressed emotions can cause panic:

- Intense emotions and feelings that have been ignored or avoided can manifest themselves through panic symptoms.
- The body can "vent" these pent-up emotions in a physical way, by releasing intense panic symptoms.

Can you identify any repressed or suppressed memories or experiences that may impact your panic response? If so, what are they? What do you remember about these experiences? How might you begin to healthily process these emotions?

_____

_____

_____

_____

_____

Societal biases and pressures

Social biases profoundly impact certain communities and, in turn, can cause panic responses. For instance, research shows that, among the LGBTQIA+ population, anxiety and panic are up to 2.5 times more common than in their gender-conforming counterparts.[3] This idea of **minority stress** is defined as individuals who are forced to deal with constant prejudice and discrimination which results in chronic stress, anxiety, and worry. Any time we deal with persistent stress, we are prone to experiencing panic.

Winnie

Winnie, a 50-year-old African American woman who identified as queer, shared a feeling that, in many situations, she was hesitant to "be herself." In certain social settings, being herself came with significant risk, so Winnie was wary of sharing her identity and fearful that it might result in discrimination or, worse, violence. Acutely aware of the realities of bias and political and ideological divisiveness in her country, Winnie could not assume that her race and sexual identity would be accepted in all settings and situations.

Winnie's panic response

Before of social or work situations where she might need to introduce herself or share details of her life, Winnie would become overwhelmed and panicky. These types of "icebreaker" activity stirred up her panic response, and she experienced panic symptoms caused by a worry that she would not be accepted when sharing the true details of her life.

Panic is often born from a place of caution, and we must recognize that this caution is not always irrational or unfounded. The underlying cause of Winnie's panic is the social narratives around minority populations. These larger social "norms" often influence how we respond emotionally to stimulus. The sad reality is that full acceptance of minority populations has yet to be widespread. Therefore, Winnie's caution was not misplaced, but her panic response was activated by this necessity to be cautious.

How societal biases and pressures can cause panic:

- Individuals from minority groups may feel they are at emotional and/or physical risk in certain social situations, which can increase feelings of fear and panic.
- Social biases can instill a sense of alienation, which can cause a panic response.

Do you feel that societal biases and pressures play a role in your panic response? If so, what are these biases and pressures and how do they affect you?

_____

_____

_____

_____

_____

Adverse childhood experiences (ACEs)

Our childhoods are the gateway to how we live and function as adults. The situations we are exposed to as young people influence how we cope with later challenges and whether we are able to do so adaptively. The idea of **adverse childhood experiences** (ACEs) is that potentially traumatic events that occur between the ages of 0 and 17 can be markers of future difficulties. These events may include:

- being a victim of violence, abuse or neglect
- witnessing violence in the home or community
- growing up in a household with substance abuse problems, mental health problems, or parental incarceration
- having a family member attempt or die by suicide
- growing up in a household with food insecurity
- experiencing homelessness or housing instability
- experiencing discrimination.[4]

Any of these ACEs may influence later experiences with anxiety and panic.

Natalie
Natalie grew up with an alcoholic mother. Her mother wavered between attempting sobriety and episodes where she would drink to the point of stupor. Natalie was never quite certain of whether she would be around "sober mom" or "drunk mom," which caused her feelings of fear and uncertainty. Sober mom was reliable and loving, whereas drunk mom was angry and judgmental. This daily uncertainty caused Natalie to live in a constant state of fear.

Natalie's panic response
On days when Natalie's mom was drinking, Natalie secluded herself in her bedroom, overcome with feelings of fear. During these times, she trembled, perspired, and found it difficult to soothe herself. Natalie's body responded to the uncertainty in the house by trying to protect itself through the release of these panic symptoms.

As she moved into adulthood, Natalie sometimes reexperienced these feelings of panic when she was in situations with individuals who were behaving in an inconsistent or aggressive manner.

How ACEs can cause panic:

- Adverse childhood events can instill a sense of danger from a young age, which can continue into adulthood and manifest through panic sensations.
- Frightening events experienced during childhood can trigger future feelings of panic.

Did you experience any adverse childhood events that may have contributed to panic? If so, which can you identify and how do you feel they have impacted your life?

_____

_____

_____

_____

_____

Family history of anxiety or panic disorder

I loved my mother, but she tended to be anxious. She was, by nature, on top of things, organized, and structured. But sometimes this led to her being overly worried. She stressed about bills being paid on time, about my brothers and I staying on top of our schoolwork, and about the household remaining in good order. She often found it difficult to relax or to be "unproductive." Parental modeling always contributes to how we navigate our lives when we become adults. This is not to suggest that our parents are to "blame" for our anxiety but, rather, that their own ways of living have some level of influence on us. As I cultivated a deeper understanding of my own issues with panic, I began to recognize that my mother's continued efforts to be productive had embedded within me. I, too, find it difficult at times to slow down or be unproductive. I also tend to play out future scenarios in my mind, which can result in anxiety and panic.

I understand the reasons why my mother was anxious: raising a family of five is not easy—there was a lot to manage and often finances were tight. With these realities in mind, part of my panic recovery has been to realize that my way of living is different than my mother's and that that is OK. I recognize the influence of how I was parented but also accept that I have the freedom to live differently. As you heal from panic, it is helpful to investigate the messages you may have consciously and unconsciously inherited from your family.

How family history can cause panic:

- Parental modeling of anxiety and stress can cause us to experience panic related to similar situations in our own lives.
- Family messages can embed into our subconscious and cause us to experience panic.

What do you notice about you family's history and behavior that may play a role in your own panic or anxiety responses? How can you begin to challenge these messages?

_____

_____

_____

_____

_____

Other contributors to panic

- **Overuse of stimulants** such as caffeine, nicotine, cocaine, methamphetamine and stimulant-based medications such as Adderall. These types of substances, by definition, stimulate the nervous system and can result in feelings of increased anxiety and panic.
- **Dehydration** can result in feelings of dizziness and lightheadedness which can be experienced as physical panic symptoms.
- **Poor work–life balance** can cause an individual's life to be constantly busy and outcome-oriented and leave little time for relaxing or restful activities. This type of lifestyle can contribute to an individual feeling overly stressed and panicked.
- **Fatigue** and poor sleep habits can exacerbate feelings of panic. When our bodies are fatigued, they respond more strongly to external stimulus.

- **Inadequate nutrition**, specifically diets that may be medically considered "unhealthy," such as those high in sugars and saturated fats, can contribute to heightened anxiety and panic symptoms.[5]
- **Environmental factors** such as living in a densely populated, heavily polluted area can heighten the body's panic response.
- **Insecure attachment** and psychological fear of abandonment can cause individuals to feel afraid when they are alone or away from others. These feelings can escalate to panic symptoms and sensations.

The power of demystification

This chapter has provided you with an understanding of many of the ways in which panic develops and where it originates from. As you continue to demystify panic, you will feel that you have more power and control over it.

Key terms

Maladaptive response: An "unhealthy" response in which an individual struggles to adapt to challenging circumstances or situations.

Adaptive response: A "healthy" response in which an individual adapts to challenging circumstances.

Vicarious trauma: Trauma that does not happen to an individual directly but that nonetheless impacts the individual's ability to cope with difficult situations.

Repressed emotions: Emotions that are subconsciously avoided or ignored.

Suppressed emotions: Emotions that are consciously avoided or ignored.

Minority stress: Stress experienced by minority groups in the form of bias and discrimination.

Adverse childhood events (ACEs): Potentially traumatic events that occur during childhood and continue to affect an individual into adulthood.

3

How panic affects daily life

Panic gets in our way. This chapter will take a look at how panic affects and disrupts our everyday lives and what we can do to reduce its disruption.

Daily functioning and activities of daily living

Our lives require us to be able to carry out certain daily tasks and activities. Panic and panic attacks can get in the way of these normally easily doable tasks. When panic sets in, activities that we had once done automatically and with ease become difficult or impossible. When we are in a constant state of fear or dread, our focus and attention turn from the tasks at hand to the perceived danger that we feel. In turn, responsibilities and obligations fall by the wayside or become de-prioritized. We can categorize these common responsibilities as **activities of daily living (ADLs)** and **daily functioning**. ADLs are essential and routine tasks that healthy individuals can carry out without assistance, whereas daily functioning refers to more general life obligations.

Activities of daily living	Daily functioning
House cleaning and home maintenance	Carrying out work/school responsibilities
Personal hygiene	Attending to personal relationships
Managing finances	Engaging in pleasurable activities/ hobbies
Shopping and meal preparation	Fulfilling family duties (parenting, etc.)
Managing communication with others	Ability to concentrate and prioritize tasks
Managing transportation[1]	Ability to balance work and personal life

Any or all of the activities listed above may be affected or inhibited by panic. Because panic, as we have discussed, often manifests through frightening physical symptoms, we can understandably become cautious or avoidant of undertaking physical tasks. This directly affects our ability to complete tasks such as house cleaning, shopping, and other ADLs. Because panic causes us to worry that we will unexpectedly experience uncomfortable physical symptoms, we may become avoidant of previously benign situations, such as attending school or work, going to social functions, or engaging in pleasurable activities. In many ways, panic robs us of full engagement with our lives.

Common responses to panic and how they affect daily life

When I was really struggling with panic attacks, I found it challenging to perform tasks that had previously been easy and done without thinking. For instance, walking my beloved Boston Terrier, Tug, became a frightening proposition. I worried that I might become dizzy and pass out while walking. The ironic part was that I loved walking my dog: it was a time of solace for me and an opportunity to engage in mindfulness. It allowed me to pay attention to my surroundings, to get fresh air and exercise, and to spend time with a beloved pet. But panic got in the way. My urge to avoid panic was so strong that sometimes I would start walking my dog, only to turn back after a few minutes as my body began to produce even the slightest frightening signals. Like many people who experience panic attacks, I became avoidant, even of activities I loved, as a way to protect myself from the possibility of having a panic attack.

My response to panic and most other responses that directly affect daily living fall into three basic categories: **constriction**, **hypervigilance**, and **numbing**. Any or all of these may be employed by a person in the aftermath of a severe panic attack. While these responses are subconsciously intended to keep us safe, they limit certain areas of our lives and daily functioning.

Constriction

When we constrict, we narrow our lives. When we aim to protect ourselves against future panic, we tend to make ourselves "small" so that nothing can harm us. Picture a child lying in the fetal position when they are frightened, arms and legs tucked into their body. In the panic mindset, the more we put ourselves out there, the more we expose ourselves to possible danger. This type of panic-driven constriction often takes the form of avoidance.

Avoidance creates an illusion of safety and is another primitive response. View it this way: a young child who is frightened may close their eyes, naively believing that, if they cannot see the scary thing, it cannot affect them. I don't mean to suggest that we are childlike or unsophisticated but that, when we're in a panic state, those basic, primitive responses kick in. Panic is complicated and can feel confusing, so a primitive response is our psyche's way of simplifying things. On the surface it seems that avoidance is a way to remain safe, when we're actually removing ourselves from our lives and restricting ourselves from experiences, relationships, and opportunities. In our quest for safety, we begin to let go of activities that we once found pleasurable, and we narrow and constrict our lives.

Constriction in action: A person who experiences a panic attack in a social setting such as a concert, for example, may decide the only way to stay safe in future similar situations is to completely avoid going to concerts. To the anxious mind, this is the only failsafe for not reexperience the severe discomfort of panic. But, rationally, this response of constriction only robs us of experiences and keeps us from the activities that we enjoy.

Hypervigilance

In simple terms, a hypervigilant response is similar to being "on guard." Like a sentry or watchman, we become highly attuned to everything that is happening in an attempt to protect against something "bad" or dangerous occurring. The problem with this response is that it causes us to devote unhealthy amounts of time and energy to being watchful. If we stayed up all night guarding our home against the possibility of an intruder, we would be exhausted and we would forgo necessary sleep. Such is the case with hypervigilant responses to panic—we put ourselves on constant watch to remain "safe" while neglecting certain vital areas of our lives.

Hypervigilance in action: Responses of a hypervigilant nature can take many forms. For example, person who has experienced a panic attack that presented in the chest and heart area may become fixated on this part of the body, constantly checking for palpitations or an accelerated heart rate. Hypervigilance takes on an obsessive nature, causing an individual to focus inordinate and unhealthy amounts of time focusing on one body part, situation, or feared stimulus. While this is happening, we ignore or deprioritize other areas of life.

Numbing

We tend to think of the concept of numbing solely in terms of substance misuse, but the reality is that we can numb ourselves in a variety of ways. From engaging in "mindless" activities that distract us from more pressing obligations to distancing ourselves from others, numbing causes us to suppress and ignore normal human emotions and feelings. Numbing can feel soothing because panic can be so intense. Sometimes feeling nothing at all can appear safer than feeling the intensity of panic. The problem with numbing is that it can result in feelings of hopelessness, purposelessness, lethargy, and depression.

Numbing in action: When I was really struggling with panic attacks, my life became very small. In addition to being hypervigilant and constricting myself, I also numbed the intense feelings by distancing myself from others and from experiences. My mind told me that I was safe only with myself in the confines of my house. But, while there, I often felt bored, lethargic, and uninspired. I did not engage in my hobbies, I let go of activities I loved, and I essentially "hunkered down" so I could feel safe. In this seemingly safe "bunker," I merely existed. This is often the result of numbing: it becomes about "getting through the day" rather than living the day.

Do you respond to panic with hypervigilance, constriction, and/or numbing? Which one(s)? How have these responses affected your daily life?

_____

_____

_____

_____

_____

Stepping back into your life

As I healed from panic and began to engage in activities I had been avoiding, I felt like I was stepping back into my life. That first walk with my dog where I was not overcome with panic was a victory. In a way, it was a return to my normal state. In psychological terms, we refer to this "normal state" of functioning as **allostasis**, or the process of maintaining **homeostasis** (when our biological systems are functioning in a stable way and are able to adapt to changing conditions).[2,3] In simple terms, it means returning to and remaining at your baseline, the place where you are able to carry out your daily activities and responsibilities without impediment. Though panic can incorrectly convince you that you will never find this baseline again, through understanding panic and learning skills to cope with it, you can victoriously return to a state of equilibrium.

What areas of you daily functioning and activities of daily living have been affected by panic? What does a return to "baseline" look like for you?

_____

_____

_____

Erica

Erica was a healthy 28-year-old. She exercised, ate a healthy diet, and took care of herself. Despite her healthy attention to her physical well-being, when she experienced feelings of physical discomfort, she tended to become overly attentive to them. Her fixation on discomfort often resulted in panic and worry about her physical health. One morning, Erica woke up and felt that it was difficult to swallow. Her throat felt tight and swollen. This feeling of discomfort triggered a larger worry that something terrible was happening physically. Throughout the day, Erica became more and more fixated on her throat, constantly checking and rechecking for changes. She was unable to focus on much else.

Daily functioning and activities of daily living can be severely impeded by panic-driven fixation. This type of fixation, while subconsciously intended to keep us safe, actually worsens our anxiety and can lead to full-blown panic as more an d more of our day-to-day life is disrupted by the stress of such focus, as illustrated in the diagram below.

Erica, for example, while fixating on her physical symptoms, was unable to focus elsewhere, becoming distracted at her job and finding it difficult to pay attention to daily tasks such as keeping on top of her bills and keeping her apartment organized. Erica's hypervigilance caused distraction and interruption of her daily life and routine.

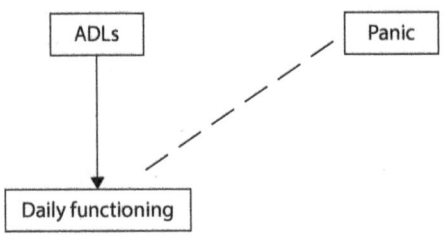

Finding the balance: attentiveness versus fixation

For Erica and those of us who struggle with panic, it can be challenging to strike a balance where we are *attentive* and *mindful* without being *fixated* or *hyperaware*. Hyperawareness tells us (incorrectly) that we are "on top of things" and that we will not "miss anything." But in truth, it is an imbalance of our attention to our lives. When we view it this way, we are able to recognize that undue attention to any one part of our daily life distracts us from other parts.

Once we recognize this panic and anxiety-based imbalance, we can work to rebalance our attention to our lives. Rebalancing for Erica allowed her to refocus on her job, her home, and her finances. As she let go of her anxious fixation, appropriate attention was restored to all aspects of her daily life.

Think for a moment whether there are any areas of your life that have become imbalanced due to panic. If so, what would rebalancing look like to you and how might it allow you to live more fully and attentively?

_____

_____

_____

_____

Common panic narratives

A natural question might be: how do we realign things and allow our lives to settle into a healthier equilibrium? First and foremost, we must accept that we are safe and not in imminent danger. Thinking in this way can be challenging, because panic works diligently to convince us otherwise. The four individuals described below are examples of how panic can embed a pattern of worry that can be difficult to break, called a **panic narrative**.

Bianca: "I'm on a hamster wheel"

Bianca's panic appeared unexpectedly, entrenching her in a cycle from which she could not escape. The more she tried to shake the feelings of panic and dread, the more they escalated, much like a hamster wheel that picks up more and more speed and is difficult to slow down. For Bianca, stepping off of this wheel felt like an impossible task and, when it was spinning uncontrollably, she struggled to focus on her job, felt exhausted, and had difficulty prioritizing tasks. The impact on her daily functioning was wide-ranging, affecting multiple areas of her life.

When "spinning," Bianca often took a sick day from her job or left work early. She didn't do this because of a lack of devotion to her work or laziness but, rather, the exhaustion brought on by panic made it impossible for her to be fully attentive to her tasks.

Bianca is not alone in describing panic as feeling like being "on a hamster wheel." Many people who experience panic feel this way. This type of exhaustion-driven response is common for individuals who experience "hamster wheel" anxiety and panic. If you ran on a treadmill past your exhaustion point, you would find it difficult to move on to the next daily task. Such is the case with Bianca's type of panic.

Affected areas of Bianca's life:

- Ability to focus attention on immediate tasks and to prioritize responsibilities
- Ability to fulfill work obligations
- Ability to be well-rested

Challenge to panic narrative

For Bianca, a change in her panic narrative is necessary for her to be able to see her panic in a different way. This may be as simple as Bianca accepting that, at times, the "hamster wheel" might speed up but that she possesses the skills and ability to step off of it and to allow herself to reset. Changes and challenges to our self-narratives are often this simple, yet they are helpful in reframing our situations and reducing the persistence of panic feelings.

Andrew: "I panic that I'll panic again"
Andrew often traveled by plane for his job. Though he never loved flying, he had never felt panicked or severely anxious about it until one very turbulent flight. On this particular flight, the captain communicated to the passengers that she was expecting severe turbulence for the duration of the flight, but that, though it would be uncomfortable, it was still safe and she knew how to navigate the atmospheric conditions.

Regardless, Andrew immediately worried. His forehead dotted with sweat. His heart rate kicked into double time. His breathing grew shallow and fast. From the moment the plane took off to the moment it landed, severe turbulence made for a bumpy ride. As the constantly unsteady plane rocked violently back and forth, Andrew realized that he had no control over the conditions.

Following this experience, Andrew began to fret about future occasions when he would be required to travel by plane. He downloaded turbulence tracking apps on his phone, did research on turbulence, and obsessively tracked the weather conditions when he had an upcoming flight.

Andrew's response to his frightening experience was to protect himself against the possibility of future similar experiences. He desperately wanted to avoid having the same type of response he had experienced on the turbulent flight—in a sense, his fear was not about turbulence so much as it was about his *response* to the turbulence. Becoming anxious about being anxious forms a mental and psychological cycle that can keep us in constant discomfort.

Affected areas of Andrew's life:

- Ability to travel without undue worry or fear
- Unhealthy amounts of time spent researching turbulence and air travel safety
- Fixation on not reexperiencing panic symptoms

Challenge to panic narrative

Andrew's narrative became one of dread: essentially that what has happened before will undoubtedly occur again. He might challenge this narrative to sound like this: "Every flight is different. Some may be turbulent and others may not. Either way, I am safe."

Suzanne: "I need to be on guard"

Suzanne was overly cautious in multiple areas of her life: at work, she was skeptical of coworkers, believing that they might not be trustworthy; at home, she often argued with her partner and was quick to assume that she was being criticized; during leisure and downtime, she would feel restless and unable to fully relax, worried that, if she was "unproductive," she might miss something important. Suzanne's tendency to be constantly "on guard" resulted in an inability to fully participate in her life.

Panic can cause us to live in a constant state of surveillance—of ourselves, of others, and of situations—because we're always on guard for things that might trigger panic. For example, if you're constantly monitoring your heart rate for acceleration, it makes it hard to be in the moment, like sitting alone with a partner at the end of the day to relax. Intense vigilance might make it difficult or impossible to enjoy a social event because you're on guard for panic triggers instead of relaxing and enjoying the company of others.

Affected areas of Suzanne's life:

- Work and relationships with coworkers
- Personal relationships/relationship with her partner
- Ability to rest and recharge

Challenge to panic narrative

It might help Suzanne to challenge her narrative of skepticism. A new, more adaptive narrative might sound like "I am careful and thoughtful but I need not be hypervigilant or overly skeptical, as that may only make me feel more anxious."

Connor: "Something bad's going to happen"

For Connor, a lingering fear that something bad—not anything specific—was bound to happen seemed to follow him through his daily life. At times, Connor's panic attached to his job, his relationships, his physical health, and his financial status, and quickly alternated between each. At other times, he was not sure what it was attaching itself to—just that he had a vague feeling of something bad potentially happening.

Panic can present in an ambiguous way, a nonspecific feeling of dread and fear that something catastrophic will occur. This is common in panic responses and is why they can feel so overwhelming and encompassing of our lives. This feeling that something bad will happen can permeate daily life and attach itself to many different situations.

Affected areas of Connor's life:

- Ability to trust himself and to believe that situations are safe and nonthreatening
- Ability to fully experience all aspects of his life
- Ability to be "present" in situations

Challenge to panic narrative

Connor may experience less panic by reframing his narrative in the following way: "Life is full of uncertainty but that does not mean it is full of danger." This gentler narrative may allow Connor to acknowledge the mysteries of life without fixating on possible negative outcomes or situations.

These common panic narratives can become powerful influences in our lives and have a significant impact on our daily functioning and ability to truly engage with life and its many opportunities and experiences. You will notice that the challenges to each individual's panic narratives allow for reframing their perspectives on the situation, which can help reduce persistent feelings of panic and dread.

What are some of the panic narratives that you feel affect you? How might you challenge and change these narratives?

_____

_____

_____

_____

_____

Complications of panic attacks and specific phobias

While Connor's type of panic was nonspecific, panic can also lead to **specific phobias**, which can cause ongoing disruptions to our daily lives. These phobias center on a certain feared situation or stimulus and are often caused by an activating event. In the example of Andrew, a single bad flight resulted in a larger fear of air travel. This is exactly the nature of complications brought on by panic attacks: they typically begin with a single stimulus or event, then extend outward into a larger, specified fear or phobia that disrupts daily life, functioning, and activities of daily living.

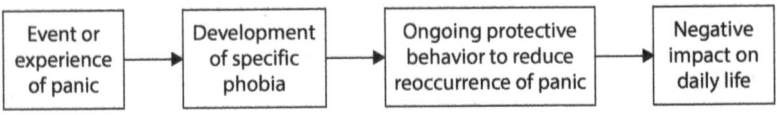

Panic attacks can be so unsettling and frightening that they can imprint within us an ongoing fear response. The specific phobias listed below may all stem from a single panic event or experience. This is the nature of panic and the way that it can continuously affect our lives and daily functioning. While not every individual who experiences panic will develop a specific phobia, the examples listed below are commonly experienced in the aftermath of a panic attack or specific panic experience.

Driving/flying phobia

A frightening experience while driving or flying can cause an individual to develop travel-related phobia, or an individual's upbringing can contribute to this type of phobia. If a parent or guardian had an irrational fear of driving or flying, it is not uncommon for their child to develop a similar fear.

Panic symptoms while driving or traveling by car are often akin to feeling overwhelmed and overstimulated. They can manifest in any of the major panic centers of the body including, but not limited to, the heart, the respiratory system, the gastrointestinal tract, and the head.

Impact on daily functioning: This type of phobia can interfere with many different components of daily life. We use some form of road, rail, or air travel for most routine activities, including work, school, shopping, and socializing. Therefore, travel-related phobias can limit daily life and have a significant impact on one's ability to fully engage in all areas of life.

Phobia of public spaces

This phobia presents as anxiety and panic that occur when an individual is in a public or crowded space from which it may be difficult to escape or exit.[4] Many people with agoraphobia become frightened that they will experience a panic attack in this type of space and be unable to escape. Ironically, agoraphobia can cause us to panic about the possibility of panicking.

Panic attacks that develop into agoraphobia often initially occur in public settings. An individual may become dizzy or lightheaded, or feel that they are going to faint in a public space such as a grocery store, mall, or office, which can trigger a larger fear of these types of settings.

Impact on daily functioning: The most common response to agoraphobia is avoidance. Individuals who become frightened in public spaces will often avoid such situations as a way to protect themselves. Avoidance, as discussed earlier, can lead to a narrowing of an individual's life as they avoid situations in order to remain "safe."

Phobia of medical settings

Individuals who have experienced medial trauma or invalidation are prone to developing a phobia of doctors and of the medical profession. For example, if a patient has felt shamed or reprimanded by a medical practitioner, they may become fearful of further invalidating experiences. Vicarious trauma can also play a role in medical phobia: a person who was present when a family member of a loved one received a frightening medical diagnosis may become themselves phobic of being in a similar situation.

Colloquially known as "white coat syndrome," the experiences of high blood pressure readings and quickened pulse rate while in a medical setting, is common among individuals who struggle with this type of phobia. For these individuals, the medical setting itself can produce a panic response in the form of increased heart rate and palpitations, sweating, labored breathing, and lightheadedness.

Impact on daily functioning: Medical phobia can result in avoidance of necessary medical maintenance such as yearly checkups and physical examinations or normal blood tests. This avoidance, while a safety-seeking measure, can actually leave patients more susceptible to medical problems going undiagnosed and untreated and can also cause individuals to avoid seeking treatment when they are ill, which can result in exacerbation of illnesses.

Phobia of illness

The vulnerability of our physical health can be a direct contributor to the development of illness-related anxiety and panic. The possibility of illness is a normal part of human existence, but a fear of getting sick can escalate to persistent fear and dread. Similar to phobia of medical settings, hypochondriasis can also arise from an individual's exposure to the illnesses of others.

Illness anxiety has, perhaps, the most direct link to panic due to its tendency to mimic more serious physical symptoms. The regions of the body that tend to exhibit panic symptoms are often the same regions where more serious medical conditions originate.

Often, people with illness anxiety fall into two groups: safety seeking or avoidant. Safety-seeking people frequently visit medical providers, which can impede daily functioning and cause a great financial strain, as they may spend large sums of money on medical treatment and seeking multiple opinions. Avoidant people might delay appointments or never make them at all, leaving themselves susceptible to illness.

Impact on daily functioning: Illness anxiety can cause significant distress on a daily basis. Illness-anxious individuals often experience persistent frightening and uncomfortable physical symptoms that mimic more serious medical problems. These symptoms commonly occur in the chest, head, gastrointestinal tract, and respiratory system, which can be misinterpreted as a serious medical condition.

Phobia of social situations

Individuals with social phobia feel uncomfortable and psychologically unsafe around others and in social settings. They experience intense physical symptoms while in social settings that include many of the criteria of a general panic attack. This can escalate to a more generalized social anxiety, in which an individual may become panicked and overwhelmed when around other people.

The exact causes of this phobia are unclear, but some experts believe that previous negative social experiences such as bullying or ostracization contribute to the development of anthropophobia. Additionally, negative responses to shyness may result in the later development of social phobia.

Impact on daily functioning: Social phobia severely inhibits an individual's ability to fully partake in their social life, resulting in avoidant behaviors, such as forgoing social events or declining to participate in social opportunities.

Phobia of fainting

A fear of fainting can also include an intense fear of physical weakness as well. Similar to illness anxiety, this phobia is specific to fainting or losing consciousness. Individuals who have fainted or experienced fainting spells may become disproportionately worried about fainting again. Ironically, as is often the case with panic, the fear of fainting can actually produce feelings of lightheadedness which can mirror and mimic an oncoming fainting spell.

Impact on daily functioning: Individuals with a phobia of fainting usually use safety-seeking avoidance. By avoiding uncomfortable social settings and situations, they may feel they are safe from experiencing a fainting spell or losing consciousness. But, as is always the case with avoidance, this type of response results in a limiting of their experiences.

Do you feel any of the specific phobias described above relate to you? If so, which one(s)? How have certain experiences impacted these fears?

_____

_____

_____

_____

_____

Panicking about panicking

In the phobias described above, you may notice a common thread: the impact on daily functioning is often a panic about reexperiencing panic. We become anxious about being anxious, a cycle from which it is difficult to escape. I recognize that when I was experiencing constant panic, I was not necessarily panicked about a certain "thing" or situation. I was panicked about becoming panicked again, about feeling those intensely uncomfortable physical symptoms, and about not knowing what was happening inside of me. I simply could not bear the thought of experiencing that discomfort again. When we begin to view panic this way, we recognize its tendency to create a vicious cycle of worry about worrying.

Do you think that your experiences with panic are sometimes related to panicking about not panicking again? If so, explain how this cycle affects you:

_____

_____

_____

_____

_____

How does understanding this cycle help you to better manage your panic response?

_____

_____

_____

_____

_____

Stepping off the wheel of anxiety and panic

Bianca's description of anxiety and panic as being on a "hamster wheel" is a common sentiment. Panic can make us feel that we are spinning and spinning tirelessly with no end result or outcome— an unending cycle of worry and dread. Though we desperately want to step off this wheel, we find it difficult because it tends to spin at an uncomfortable rate of speed. While Part II of this book will discuss ways to cope with this feeling of spinning your wheels, the understanding of the underlying causes that you have gained through the first part of this book will help you to begin to feel power over the discomfort of panic.

This comprehension of underlying causes allows us to slow down the wheel of worry and to create more room in our lives for elements that had been deprioritized by panic. Walking my dog without worrying that I would experience a catastrophic medical emergency, driving to a social event without fear that something terrible will happen as we travel, or taking in a movie or concert without an assumption of impending doom: our lives open up when we step out of this "hamster wheel."

Restoration of daily functioning

Once we understand the ways in which panic affects our daily functioning, our goal becomes to seek ways to restore healthy daily functioning. Whether this means Andrew taking a flight without anxious fixation, or Erica worrying less about her physical health, this return to our daily lives allows us to realign priorities, fully engage in all aspects of our lives, and live in a less constant state of worry. We once again become able to engage healthily in the activities of daily living and our daily functioning returns to a state of equilibrium.

Signs of restored daily functioning:

- Fulfillment of work/school duties and obligations
- Ability to create a healthy work–life balance
- Positive social and personal relationships
- Restored interest in leisure activities and hobbies
- Proper attention to personal hygiene and self-care[5]

What elements of your daily functioning and activities of daily living would you like to work to restore through your process of learning to cope with and heal from panic? For me, a simple one was being able to walk my dog without fear of something bad happening. Think about how might your life improve by being able to restore these elements.

Key terms

Activities of daily living (ADLs): Essential and routine tasks that healthy individuals can carry out without assistance.

Daily functioning: Common obligations of life such as work and family responsibilities and duties.

Hypervigilance: A panic response in which an individual becomes overly watchful and attentive in order to protect themselves from perceived harm or danger.

Constriction: A panic response in which an individual "narrows" their life and lets go of previously important activities in order to feel safe from reexperiencing panic.

Numbing: A panic response in which an individual suppresses or ignores normal feelings and emotions as a safety behavior.

Allostasis: The process by which the body responds to stressors in order to regain equilibrium.

Homeostasis: The state of stable equilibrium maintained by the body and the physiological systems.

Panic narrative: Stories that we tell ourselves that influence our tendency to experience panic.

Specific phobia: Panic centered on a certain feared situation or stimulus (such as flying or driving) and often caused by an activating event.

Part II
Coping with panic

This part of the book will help you learn methods, skills, and strategies for working to overcome panic and reduce its impact on your life. Though it may not always feel like it, panic *can* be tamed and we can learn ways to cope with it and to take away its power. The skills you will learn throughout this chapter will be applicable throughout your life and will hopefully be an empowering and helpful part of your healing journey.

4
Self-care and panic

Just as our daily functioning can be negatively affected by panic, so can our ability to care for ourselves and to direct healthy attention toward our well-being. Self-care as a general concept means taking care of ourselves just as lovingly and compassionately as we would a beloved pet, infant, or loved one. Panic can so intensely focus our attention elsewhere that it can cause us to let go of and deprioritize our own self-care. This can negatively affect our daily lives and lead to uncomfortable consequences such as constant fatigue, physical pain, emotional distress, and inattention to pleasurable parts of our lives. Part of healing from panic is reprioritizing yourself and your life.

Self-compassion

Self-care can happen only if we have self-compassion. If we do not feel love or affection for something, we will not be committed to taking care of it. So, self-care truly begins with viewing ourselves with love and compassion and believing that we are deserving of kind and gentle attention and soothing. As you continue on your journey of healing from panic, ask yourself whether you have been kind and loving toward yourself. If you recognize that you are sometimes hard on yourself or harsh toward yourself, think about how you might send yourself a different, more compassionate message. Self-statements and mantras of self-compassion might sound like this:

- "I am deserving of peace."
- "Especially when my life is difficult, I treat myself kindly and lovingly."
- "I allow myself to ask for help and support when I need it."
- "I see myself as valuable and important even in difficult times."

Releasing panic shame

When we panic, we often tell ourselves we are broken, and somehow less adept at living than others. Researcher and author Brené Brown describes shame as "the intensely painful feeling or experience of believing we are flawed and therefore unworthy of acceptance and belonging."[1]

When we accept that we deserve love and peace, we can work to let go of feelings of shame and humiliation that often accompany anxiety and panic. When we recognize and accept that worry, anxiety, and panic are not markers of abnormality but instead are commonly experienced feelings, we view ourselves less harshly and judgmentally. This shift in self-perspective helps us turn toward healing.

Buddhist teacher Thích Nhất Hạnh encourages us to view our most intense emotions as a "howling baby" that needs soothing and comforting.[2] Just as a baby or infant would not be soothed or comforted by a loud, harsh, or aggressive response, neither will our feelings of panic. If we shame ourselves for feeling anxious, we are likely to continue experiencing the feeling rather than finding any relief.

Unfortunately, cultural and societal messaging does not always encourage extending grace toward ourselves when we are struggling. Rather, it sometimes tells us to "suck it up," "be tough," or remember that others "have it worse." This type of message serves only to reinforce our sense of shame.

Shame release

Take a moment here to be gentle with yourself. Sit quietly and comfortably and remind yourself that you are not broken because you experience panic. Remember that self-compassion is more healing than harsh self-judgment. Repeat these reminders to yourself:

- "When I feel panicky, I need compassion and comfort."
- "Panic is uncomfortable but it does not define me."
- "I am actively working to lessen the impact of panic on my life."
- "Anxiety and panic are common. I am not broken because I experience panic at times."

Self-talk and panic

In moments of panic, I have yelled at myself—my inner voice screaming at the top of its lungs—STOP PANICKING! YOU'RE FINE! CALM DOWN! As loud as this voice can be, it has never actually helped me to calm down or feel less panicky. We are always talking to ourselves. We possess an inner monologue that runs on throughout our day, giving us constant—often unsolicited—feedback. Though it may not always feel this way, we can exert some level of control over this often unhelpful inner voice. Have you ever listened to something someone said and thought to yourself, "I don't agree with that at all"? You are allowed to question your own inner voice just as you sometimes question the statements and opinions of others. Your inner voice is not always accurate, and it is a skill to be able to question it and to decide not to take it at its word.

When we experience panic, our self-messaging is often accusatory and punishing. We ask ourselves questions like: "What's wrong with me?", "Why am I being ridiculous?", and "Why can't I be normal?" We would never say things like this to others, but we readily say them to ourselves and rarely question their accuracy or helpfulness. Just as a coach who yells and demeans is often less effective than a supportive coach, our self-talk, too, is more helpful when it is gentle and understanding. Here are some common examples of both unhelpful and helpful self-talk:

Unhelpful self-talk	Helpful self-talk
"Toughen up."	"It's OK to slow down right now."
"Don't be a baby"	"I feel panicky right now and that's OK"
"You're being ridiculous."	"Worry is a normal emotion."
"Other people go through worse"	"Many people experience anxiety and panic."

Take a moment to consider whether your self-talk is harsh or compassionate when you're experiencing panic. How could you change your self-talk so that it's more helpful in moments when you're feeling panicky?

Self-soothing

As children, most of us relied on our parents and caregivers to soothe us when we felt uncomfortable. Our parents cared for our wounds, both physical and emotional, and we felt safe knowing that we could go to them for soothing and reassurance. We felt taken care of and protected from harm. As we move through life, however, this reliance naturally turns toward ourselves: we become able to soothe ourselves and to find comfort from within when we're distressed or overwhelmed. We all possess the ability to self-soothe, even if we have had inadequate soothing from parents and caregivers. This ability continues to develop throughout our lives.

In times of panic, however, we can easily forget that we have the ability to self-soothe. When we are young, it is easy: go to our parents or caregivers and they will know what to do. It is more complex for adults. An active and continued effort to recognize what we need and what helps us when we are panicked allows us to access our self-soothing skills when we need them. I can identify three distinct things that I need when I'm feeling panicked:

1 **Stillness and rest.** My type of panic makes everything feel like it's moving too quickly. So, in these moments, I have found that finding a moment of stillness is helpful in returning to my baseline. This can simply mean sitting down or momentarily ceasing movement.

2 **Speaking my feelings.** When I panic, I feel full with emotion and energy. If I hang on to all of this myself, I begin to feel even more escalated, uncomfortable, and panicky. I have found that it is helpful for me to be able to share what I am experiencing with someone. This can be as simple as telling a loved one that "I am feeling panicky." Sharing this allows me a sense of relief, and I feel soothed by doing so.

3 **Deep breathing.** I tend to feel short of breath when I am in a panic state. It can feel difficult to catch my breath, and my respiration feels pressured and tight. In these moments, a deep breath that I inhale through my nose and exhale out of my mouth helps me to feel grounded. It serves to restore my breathing to a normal cadence and rhythm and, in doing so, reduces other panic sensations such as lightheadedness and feelings of disequilibrium.

Figuring out what I need when I'm feeling panicky took time and attention. But once I had a clear sense of simple things that helped, I felt I had gained specific tools that I could access when needed. Your ability to self-soothe relies on developing an awareness of what helps you specifically. A helpful way to begin this exploration is to ask yourself: *What do I need when I am feeling panicky?* As you consider your answer to this question, keep it simple as I have done in my three needs, described above. For example, things like taking a walk, stepping outside, or sitting quietly might help create a sense of calm.

Identify three or four simple things that you think would help when you are experiencing panic:

_____

_____

_____

_____

The skill of self-soothing is knowing what is available to you and how to use it. You wouldn't hammer a nail with pliers—similarly, understanding which tools are not helpful can ensure that the ones you go to are the ones that will help the most. Just as I know what does help me when I am feeling panicky, I know what does not. Self-shaming, harsh self-talk, and frustration with myself are not helpful. Be sure you have a sense of what does not help you to feel soothed so that you can avoid those options and use more effective ones.

Daily self-care to reduce panic

Now that you have reprioritized yourself and remembered to treat yourself with compassion, you can think about what type of care you need when you are feeling panic. When we care for ourselves, we are less apt to experience chaotic physical symptoms and sensations, just as a vehicle that is well-maintained is less likely to break down. Self-care is a daily endeavor, requiring attention to our needs, both biological and psychological. We can break down self-care into the following three categories: physical, mental, and emotional. When we understand what we uniquely require in each category, we ensure that we can maintain a state of equilibrium and that we are not overly susceptible to intense and extreme emotions such as panic.

Physical:

- Adequate rest and sleep
- Adequate nutrition and hydration
- Exercise, movement, and physical activity
- Moderation of stimulant and depressant substances such as caffeine, alcohol, and marijuana

Mental:

- Engagement in mentally stimulating activities
- Work experience that is satisfying and challenging
- Curiosity and interest in learning
- Healthy work–life balance

Emotional:

- Connection to others and attention to social relationships
- Allowance of feelings and emotions rather than suppression of feelings
- Hobbies and activities that provide pleasure and allow for relaxation
- Employment of healthy coping skills and strategies

When these elements of self-care are firmly in place, we are able to live in a state of relative equilibrium. Though we may experience problems and challenges, we have the ability to navigate them healthily and to return to "baseline" without spiraling into an intense or unmanageable emotional response. However, when these elements are lacking, we find that we more easily slip into feelings like panic. Think of it in terms of atmospheric conditions: when skies are calm and there are no disruptions in the atmosphere, the weather is pleasant and serene. When, however, there is a disruptive system or pattern in the atmosphere, conditions are ripe for storms or turbulent weather. When our self-care is in place without disruption, the conditions allow for equilibrium in our lives. Use the self-care self-assessment below to help you work whether you are self-care ready.

Self-assessment: self-care

Think about self-care at this point in your life. If you feel it's lacking, do not despair—you can always improve and be more dedicated to ensuring your daily well-being. On the self-rated scale below, consider each element of your daily self-care and make an honest assessment. Notice where you might like to pay more attention or work to improve in order to create a better equilibrium.

I get adequate rest and sleep:

1 (not at all true)   2   3   4   5 (definitely true)

I get adequate nutrition and hydration:

1   2   3   4   5

I make time for exercise and physical activity:

1   2   3   4   5

I moderate the use of stimulant and depressant substances:

1   2   3   4   5

I engage in mentally stimulating activities:

1   2   3   4   5

My work is satisfying and challenging:

1   2   3   4   5

I maintain a healthy work–life balance:

1   2   3   4   5

I try to connect with others and to maintain healthy social relationships:

1   2   3   4   5

I allow myself to feel my emotions rather than to suppress or ignore them:

1   2   3   4   5

I engage in hobbies and activities that bring me pleasure and allow me to relax:

1   2   3   4   5

I try to limit my exposure to negative, violent, and triggering media:

1   2   3   4   5

I use healthy coping skills and strategies for dealing with difficult situations and emotions:

1   2   3   4   5

Based on your honest self-assessment, are there any areas where you would like to work to improve your self-care? If so, what are they and how do you plan to pay more attention to these areas?

_____

_____

_____

_____

_____

Creating and maintaining balance in your life

As described above, an unbalanced atmosphere creates conditions in which storms occur. The same goes for an unbalanced life: when things are off-kilter and misaligned, conditions can quickly become turbulent and we can find ourselves feeling untethered and at the mercy of the storm. One of the main ways our lives become imbalanced is in our relationships with our jobs. Because we want to do well at our jobs, we often pay them a great deal of attention, sometimes to the detriment of other areas of our lives. When we focus too much on work, we become more susceptible to stress, worry, fixation, and panic related to our jobs. In seeking to create a balance between our jobs and the rest of our lives, it is necessary to create specific boundaries. Statements of these boundaries might include:

- Work is a part of my life, not my whole life.
- My bed/couch/armchair, etc. is for rest, not for work.

- I am unavailable for work-related issues after a certain time of the day.
- I have a finite, not a limitless, amount of energy that I can devote to work.

Write down what boundaries you would like to remind yourself of in regard to your job:

_____

_____

_____

The importance of balance in our lives extends beyond our relationships with our jobs. Our lives can become imbalanced in various ways; being mindful of maintaining a healthy balance is a part of ensuring that we do not make ourselves vulnerable to overwhelm. Some other areas where balance is important are in the table below.

Area	Example of balance
Relationships	healthy time for yourself, your family, others in your social circle
Devices and media	balance with video games, phone scrolling, social media
The news cycle	being mindful of the psychological impact of constant exposure to tragic or frightening stimulus
Time management	ensuring that adequate time is devoted to important areas of life
Tasks	balancing life obligations and responsibilities
Emotions	creating time and space for emotions and feelings; not suppressing them in order to focus on other things

Picture life balance as a seesaw; if there is too much on weight on one side, the entire mechanism will become unstable. For example, if you have an unhealthy balance with your job, your seesaw might become so unbalanced that everything outside of your job no longer carries the weight or the importance that it deserves.

• Everything else (relationships, leisure, self-care, ADLs, etc.)

• Thinking about work after hours
• Answering calls and emails at all hours of the day
• Prioritizing work over other parts of life
• Worrying and fixating about work

Think about your life balance. Where would you like to make changes to ensure that you are creating conditions for equilibrium? What needs to be rebalanced?

_____

_____

_____

_____

_____

The importance of rest and leisure

True balance in our lives includes our willingness to rest and to engage in pleasurable activities. Society sometimes gets in the way of allowing ourselves to stop, slow down, and relax. In a culture seemingly obsessed with the virtues of productivity and busyness, resting can be a radical act. But rest is vital in managing anxiety, panic, and overwhelm. If we run at full speed all the time, we are bound to crash, which can easily take the form of panic.

Robin
Robin, a high school history teacher and soccer and basketball coach, consistently worked an 80-hour week. After school, she would rush to practice for one of the sports she coached. Her normal workday began at 6:00 a.m. and ended around 9:00 p.m. Once home, Robin would hurriedly eat dinner, shower, and get ready for bed. Weekends were

typically occupied with games, tournaments, and practices for her teams. The idea of rest or of not being busy was completely foreign to Robin.

On the sidelines during a soccer game, Robin began to feel dizzy. She thought she might faint and a feeling of fear washed over her. She had never experienced a panic attack before so she was not sure what to make of this feeling. Robin decided to let the other coaches know she was not feeling well and headed home early. Once there, she sat on the couch in silence, slowly feeling that she was OK.

This is a panic attack that results from overwhelm. When we do not allow for adequate time to rest, our physical systems let us know—and often not in a subtle way. Robin's body, through its panicked response, was screaming for rest. Once she removed herself from the overwhelming situation and rested, the panic symptoms dissipated. View it this way:

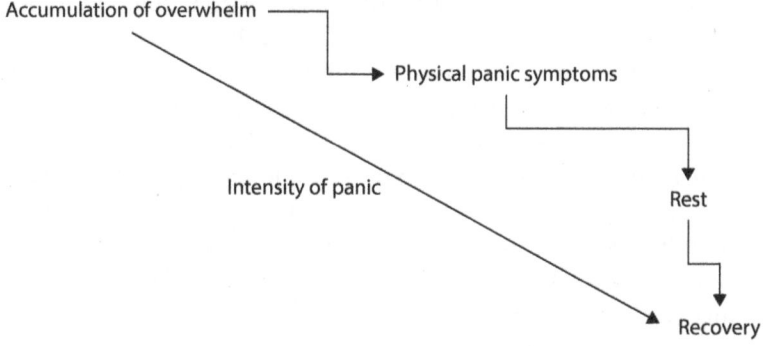

Like many individuals who overwork themselves, Robin may have avoided this intense physical response had she made a more sustained effort to incorporate rest into her busy schedule. The irony and frustration of panic is that, often, it is only after we experience it that we begin to recognize what we need to do to create a healthier balance in our lives. Robin, in the wake of this panic experience, became acutely aware that she was taking on too much, and that she needed to find ways to balance her life and work in a more effective way by incorporating rest into her daily life.

Rest and leisure can take many different forms. A social myth tells us that self-care comes only in the form of a day at the spa or a long vacation. In reality, we can allow ourselves to rest even within the framework of a busy day. Robin began to make time to slow down in simple ways: she built a lunch break into her schedule (something she had not done in her 20 years of teaching), she began to opt out of certain nonessential practices for her teams, and she made an effort to give herself wind-down time prior to rushing off to bed after getting home. These seemingly simple changes helped Robin to avoid reaching a point of overwhelm that resulted in panic.

Leisure is often less valued than productivity in our society. But, physically and psychologically, leisure activities are every bit as important. In fact, they have a direct impact on one another: if we do not allow for enough rest, we cannot be productive, and if we are too productive, we are unable to rest.

Robin, by allowing herself to rest and slow down, was also able to reincorporate certain pleasurable activities that she had forgotten about in her overscheduled life. During her lunch breaks, she would listen to music (something she loved but often did not do when she was overwhelmed); on evenings when she bypassed practices, she and her partner would make popcorn and watch a movie; before bed, she would sit quietly and allow herself to release the energy and emotions of the day. These activities, while seemingly mindless, are productive if we reframe how we see productivity; leisure activities help to create a healthier life balance and to reduce feelings of overwhelm.

What are some pleasurable leisure activities that might help you to rest and to reduce the potential for overwhelm and panic?

_____

_____

_____

_____

_____

Letting go of perfectionism

I often hear from clients, and have said myself, "I just want to *never* be anxious." This type of perfectionist thinking serves only to leave us feeling disappointed in ourselves when we fall short of our self-imposed high bar. The idea of *never* experiencing anxiety is like never feeling sad or angry: not only is it impossible, but it would also be strange and would cheapen the wide range of human emotions.

While we can accept anxiety as a commonly experienced feeling, we do not have to feel that we are ruled by it. The power of acceptance is that it relieves us of unreasonable expectations of ourselves. Think of an athlete who experiences performance anxiety because her standards and expectations of herself are so unreasonably high. She feels that any slipup or misstep is unacceptable and, therefore, becomes unable to perform at the high level at which she performs when not in a perfectionist mindset. The same happens when we tell ourselves we must never be anxious: life becomes difficult to navigate and we do not function at our optimal level.

Letting go of perfectionist expectations of ourselves requires honest acceptance of the commonality of difficult feelings such as panic. Here are some things to recognize as you work to release yourself from unreasonable self-standards:

- Our lives and the world in which we live are complex and complicated, therefore anxiety and panic are not abnormal or unacceptable feelings.
- It is impossible to live a life in which we never experience fear or anxiety.
- An expectation that we will never feel anxious is unrealistic and unattainable.
- Unreasonable standards for ourselves often result in feelings of disappointment and failure.

Asking for help and support

Part of self-care is a willingness to ask for help when we need it. Though we have the ability to self-soothe, situations arise when the support of others is helpful. I mentioned earlier that one of the things that helps me when I am feeling panicky is sharing my feelings with someone. When I speak what I am feeling, the intensity of the feeling almost instantly lessens. On these occasions, I am not necessarily looking for the other person to provide solutions but, rather, simply to feel that I am not alone with my discomfort. Every human being can understand and relate to feelings of anxiety and worry, so our willingness to share these feelings can help us to feel less isolated. The following mantras may help you to remember that it is OK to share even your most uncomfortable feelings, and that this willingness to share may help you to cope:

- "It is OK for me to share how I am feeling, even when the feelings are intense, difficult, and overwhelming."
- "Sharing is a way for me to release accumulated feelings and to reduce their intensity."
- "Feeling less isolated and alone is a way for me to cope with my discomfort."

Therapy and medication

When panic begins to severely disrupt our lives, psychotherapy and medication are options that can help us cope. It can feel uncomfortable to start therapy or begin taking medication, but doing either or both can be supportive factors in recovery from panic. As always, do what is right for you and what you are comfortable with; this section is intended simply to help you understand how therapy and medication may be helpful in dealing with panic.

Psychotherapy, typically one-on-one sessions with a credentialed mental health professional, can help you to develop a trusted relationship with someone who understands the psychology behind anxiety and panic and who can help you learn skills and strategies for coping with panic. Psychologists, licensed counselors, social workers, or other credentialed professionals can fill this role. In my personal journey, therapy was extremely valuable and helpful; it taught me to understand what panic is, why it happens, and what I could do about it. Further, it gave me a safe and confidential space to talk things out, to unburden heavy and intense emotions, and feel a sense of relief and healing. Therapy helped me to feel I had an additional layer of support for what had become a very difficult part of my life.

Medication can also be a helpful option for coping with panic. While there is sometimes a negative stigma associated with taking medication for anxiety or panic, there is also a proven record of success regarding antianxiety medications. These medications can help people struggling with panic and panic attacks return to the "baseline" described earlier.

The most commonly prescribed medications for panic are **selective serotonin reuptake inhibitors (SSRIs)**. SSRIs increase serotonin (a natural body chemical that affects mood) levels in the brain, allowing for stabilization of mood and a reduction in anxiety and panic. These medications typically cause little or no side effects and have been proven safe and effective.

While other types of medications may be prescribed for anxiety and panic, the best course of action is to contact a psychiatrist or prescriber to discuss the best options for you based on your unique experience. Here are some common medication myths to keep in mind to ensure you keep your options open:

Myth	Fact
Medication will turn me into a "zombie" and I won't be myself.	Antianxiety medications such as SSRIs do not alter our personalities or "numb" us out.
Medication is only for severely mentally ill people.	Medication can benefit many people, not only those with severe mental illnesses.
I will experience severe side effects.	For most people, there are either no side effects or very minimal side effects.
I will become reliant on medication or unable to function without it.	SSRIs do not have addictive qualities and do not result in reliance.
My only option for panic is to go on medication.	Medication is just one supportive factor in managing panic. While it may be helpful for some, it is not for everyone.

A combination of psychotherapy and medication is effective for many people who struggle with panic. Being open to these options can help you to feel that there are various supportive factors that can help with panic.

Creating a self-care plan

Create a plan for how you can implement the safe-care strategies discussed in this chapter to help you to feel prepared for coping with uncomfortable feelings of overwhelm, worry, and panic. This plan is divided into five categories: self-talk, self-soothing, life balance, leisure, and supportive factors. The sample plan is from my own life and includes the actual strategies and applications that I use to help me when I am feeling panicked. It is followed by a blank plan that you can fill out and use to help you.

Phil's (author) self-care plan

Self-talk

My intentions: To make a sustained and conscious effort to speak to myself kindly and compassionately, especially when I am feeling panicky.

Specific actions: Change the inner wording and language I use with myself when I feel panicky. Ensure that my language is gentle, compassionate, and soothing.

Practical application: When I feel panicky, I will tell myself "You are feeling anxious right now and that is OK," instead of what I usually tell myself, which is "Stop panicking, you're being ridiculous."

Self-soothing

My intentions: To work to be able to soothe myself when I am experiencing panic by using self-care strategies.

Specific actions: Implement a grounding exercise when I am feeling emotionally escalated or panicky.

Practical application: Take a deep breath through my nose and exhale out of my mouth in moments of overwhelm.

Life balance

My intentions: To devote less time to work and more time to activities that I enjoy.

Specific actions: I would like to listen to music and read more often. Also, I would like to spend more time with my family.

Practical application: Ensure that I schedule my last session of the day so that I have time for myself and my family, and to wind down and decompress. My last session will be at 6:00 p.m. no matter what.

Leisure

My intentions: I would like to reengage in hiking with my dog, which is something I love to do and used to do more frequently.

Specific actions: Build time into my schedule for being able to travel to a trail and hike with my dog.

Practical application: Rather than getting lost in other obligations or pressuring myself to be "productive," following through on my promise to myself to hike with my dog more often.

Supportive factors

My intentions: To be sure that I consistently attend therapy to help me continue to manage anxiety and panic; to explore medication for coping with panic.

Specific actions: Speaking to my therapist about scheduling a standing appointment; setting up a consultation with a psychiatrist to discuss medication.

Practical application: Continuing with therapy; beginning to take an SSRI medication to help me with anxiety and panic.

Below, you can create your own plan to help you when you are feeling panicky

My self-care plan

Self-talk

My intentions:

_____

_____

Specific actions:

_____

_____

Practical application:

_____

_____

Self-soothing

My intentions:

_____

_____

Specific actions:

_____

_____

Practical application:

_____

_____

Life balance

My intentions:

_____

_____

Specific actions:

_____

_____

Practical application:

_____

_____

Leisure

My intentions:

_____

_____

Specific actions:

_____

_____

Practical application:

_____

_____

Supportive factors

My intentions:

_____

_____

Specific actions:

_____

_____

Practical application:

_____

_____

5

Mindfulness strategies for panic

Self-care and mindfulness go hand in hand. When we care for ourselves, we are present in our lives and attentive to what is happening around and within us. Simply defined, mindfulness means being aware, paying attention, and being "present." Mindfulness can help us to let go of thoughts and fixations on what *might* happen, what *could* go wrong, or what we're missing. When we are mindful, we live our lives based on the here and now rather than on the what might be.

Panic as a future thought

When we tie panic to the future, we understand how unhelpful it is to us in the present moment. Making inaccurate and often frightening predictions about future scenarios, without evidence, logic, or rationality, does nothing for us. But these predictions can be so convincing that we often find ourselves lost in the uncertainty and dread of the "what if." The anxious and panicky mind thrives in uncertainty, creating scenarios and causing our bodies to respond intensely and primitively.

So, how do we remain in the present and avoid losing ourselves in future thoughts? Being present isn't always an easy task, but it is doable through sustained and daily effort. Once we recognize that we are spending an awful lot of time thinking about future scenarios, we can turn our attention toward the present. The future hasn't happened yet, but the present is always occurring. And the more we pay attention to it, the more we feel peaceful, at ease, and safe—the very feelings that panic robs us of.

Use the self-assessment below to understand whether you over-focus on the the future:

Self-assessment: worrying about the future

Think about how much time you spend thinking about, worrying about, and playing out future scenarios, many of which will never actually happen. Complete the self-assessment below to help you begin to recognize where there is room for turning toward the present.

I spend a great deal of time thinking about what might happen:
1 (not at all true)   2   3   4   5 (definitely true)

I often play out and "rehearse" future scenarios in my head:
1   2   3   4   5

It is sometimes difficult for me to be fully engaged in what is happening in the moment:
1   2   3   4   5

I often feel frightened and overwhelmed by not knowing what will happen in the future:
1   2   3   4   5

My feelings of anxiety, worry, and panic are usually about what *might* happen, not about what *is* happening:
1   2   3   4   5

Many of future scenarios that I play out in my head never come to fruition:
1   2   3   4   5

I think that, if I were more present, I would feel less panicky:
1   2   3   4   5

"What if" versus "What is"

If, through your honest self-assessment, you have realized that you spend a lot of time thinking about the future, it may be helpful to make a clear distinction between "what if" and "what is." Usually, "what ifs" enter our minds in the form of questions, whereas "what is" thoughts take the form of statements. "What ifs" are maybes, "possiblys," and "potentiallys." They are vague, inaccurate, and often of a catastrophic nature. Returning to my previous example of walking my dog, here is the difference between a mind full of what ifs and a mind that pays attention to what is:

What if:

- "*What if* a car comes out of nowhere and strikes me or my dog?"
- "*What if* it starts to storm while we are far from home?"
- "*What if* I don't get back home in time to get ready for work?"

What is:

- "*It is* very warm and sunny today."
- "My dog *is* enjoying this walk and sniffing everything in sight."
- "*It is* early spring and many of these trees *are* beginning to bloom."

As simple as this notion may seem, think about how frequently we are somewhere else in our own heads. My "what if" thoughts described above do nothing more than take me out of the present experience of walking my dog on a sunny day in early spring, surrounded by blooming trees. You can probably see how these "what if thoughts can easily escalate—they tend to be anxiety-driven to begin with, so it is not a far leap from them to cross over into panic thoughts and uncomfortable physical responses.

Just notice

Wherever you are as you are reading this book, take a look around. Notice—*really notice*—your surroundings. Slowly and attentively scan the room or the area where you are right now. Don't latch your vision or your thoughts on to any one item or element. Just *notice*. As you notice, remember to try not to add analysis, meaning, or conclusions to what you see. Remember, this practice of just noticing can help you to reduce feelings of panic about what *might* happen and remind you to pay attention to what *is* happening.

How did it feel to "just notice"? Do you think that making a sustained effort to be in the "here and now" will help you to feel less panicky? How so? How do you intend to remain more present in your daily life?

Grounding techniques

Panic can feel like we have lost our footing. When we panic, we often feel unmoored, lightheaded, and no longer tethered to the earth. In moments of intense panic, we may even feel that we are not in our own bodies. Grounding techniques can help us to regain a sense of stabilization. The four simple grounding techniques described below can help you to restabilize during moments of panic and overwhelm.

- **Soft touch:** Run your hands and fingers slowly and gently across a surface. As you do this, simply pay attention to the feel of your skin on the surface. Mindfulness is all about attention and this grounding technique allows you to refocus your attention by using your sense of touch.
- **Heartspace:** The body's intense panic responses can be calmed by offering ourselves physical comfort. When a newborn baby has a startle response upon being placed in her bassinet, she may be soothed by her parent gently placing their hand upon her chest, above her heart. In this "heartspace," we feel comforted and soothed. You can soothe your body by gently placing both hands on your chest, above the area of your heart and taking a deep, soothing breath. Often, this gentle comfort immediately reduces feelings of panic and fear.
- **Dropping anchor:** In this grounding technique, we use our bodies to remind ourselves that we are safe, secure, and rooted. Just as an anchor keeps a vessel steady and in place during a storm, anchoring ourselves allows us to feel stable in times of

stress. We use the acronym ACE to help guide us through the dropping anchor technique:

Acknowledge
Come back
Engage

First, *acknowledge* how you are feeling and how your body is responding to your feelings. Next, *come back* into your body, which you can do in a variety of ways: for some people, a simple deep breath in through the nose and out through the mouth allows for a return to the body. For others, a stretch or movement of the arms and legs does the trick. The idea is to feel your body and bring yourself back into your physical being. Last, *engage* in what you are doing. This is the act of noticing and of returning to a state of presence in the moment. By employing this technique, you will feel more anchored and grounded.[1]

- **54321:** This technique encourages you to engage your five senses as a way to ground yourself and to return to the present moment – give it a go here.

54321

Begin by identifying five things you can see. Next, identify four things you can touch, then three things you can hear. Finish by identifying two things you can smell and one thing you can taste. This practice of mindful attention is helpful in returning to what is actually happening around you in this moment.

Five things you can see:

1 _____

2 _____

3 _____

4 _____

5 _____

Four things you can touch:

1 _____

2 _____

3 _____

4 _____

Three things you can hear:

1 _____

2 _____

3 _____

Two things you can smell:

1 _____

2 _____

One thing you can taste:

1 _____

You can employ these grounding techniques at any moment in your day. You do not need to be in a specific place in order to implement these strategies. Because panic can come upon us unexpectedly, it is helpful to carry with us immediately accessible tools that we can use at a moment's notice. Grounding techniques are a vital part of your coping toolbox.

Breathwork

Our breath and how we breathe during moments of panic and emotional escalation can make all the difference in how quickly we're able to return to a grounded state. Breathwork is more complex than just "taking a deep breath" when we're panicked. The three simple types of breathwork described below will help you to use your breathing as a tool for grounding and reducing intense feelings of panic.

- **Buddha breath:** In the sacred Buddhist text *Ānāpānasati Sutta,* attention to breath is described as one of the keys of mindfulness. This type of breathing begins in the abdomen and follows with deep inhalation and slow exhalation. First, breathe in deeply, filling your abdomen and belly. Next, release a long, slow exhalation out of your mouth and then close your mouth. The inhalations and exhalations that follow will be through your nose.

  As you breathe this way, simply pay attention to your breath. If your mind wanders, allow your attention to return to your breaths, in and out, in and out. This type of breathing will help you to slow down and focus your attention on your breath rather than on other distractions and worries.

- **The tip of the nose:** It can be challenging to keep our focus on our breath. By paying attention, not to our abdomen or lungs, but rather to the tip of the nose, we can direct our focus to the breath as it goes in and out. As you breathe, pay attention to the sensations in the nose and the nostril as you breathe. The more you are able to focus your attention, the less you will find it attached to other thoughts. This is the power of breathwork and how it can help to reduce feelings of anxiety and panic.

- **Box breathing:** This is a simple strategy for using your breath to ground and calm you. The diagram below illustrates how to practice the box breathing method:

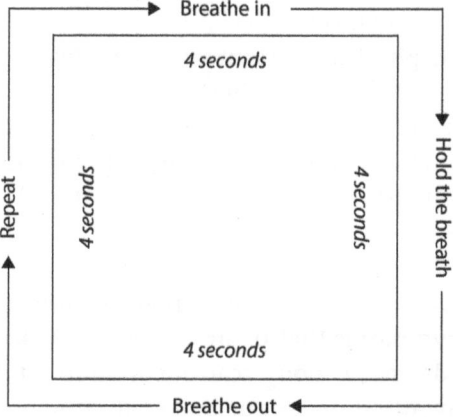

- By taking 4 seconds each to breathe in, hold the breath, breathe out, and repeat the process, your body will begin to slow down and you will feel recentered and stabilized. This type of breathing can also slow down your respiration and heart rate in moments of panic.

Meditation

Many people incorrectly define meditation as "having no thoughts" or sitting in complete and absolute peace and stillness. In reality, meditation is more about pulling ourselves out of the past or the future, and returning to the present moment. Recognize the following myths about meditation so that you feel that you can successfully implement a meditation practice and let go of popular, yet untrue, sentiments about meditating.

Meditation myths

- You have to practice Buddhism to meditate.
- Meditation takes hours, and most people simply don't have enough time.
- Meditation is just a self-care "fad."
- Meditation means not thinking about anything and that's impossible.
- Meditation means just sitting there and not doing anything.

The reality of meditation is that it can be a tool for coping with emotional and physical discomfort. It can teach us to tap into peace and stillness at times when we are surrounded by mental noise and discord. The six types of mediations described below will help you to begin building a meditation practice that you can use to help you in times of panic and overwhelm.

Body scan

Panic can cause our bodies to feel intensely uncomfortable, and the physical symptoms that panic causes can make us feel frightened and in danger. A body scan meditation allows us to slow down and pay attention to our bodies in a helpful, rather than anxious, way. When we panic, we tend to pay anxious attention to our bodies, checking them for discomfort and fixating on certain physical areas and sensations. This type of attention actually escalates feelings of panic. A body scan meditation, on the other hand, encourages gentle and compassionate attention to our bodies, and helps us to recognize that we are safe and healthy in this moment. This gentle attention and recognition slows our racing thoughts and our unhelpful focus on physical sensations. The following body scan meditation illustrates how to use gentle attention in order to quell panic feelings.

Find a comfortable position where you feel at ease and safe. Begin by taking a deep breath, feeling relaxed as you exhale. Gently close your eyes and turn your attention inward, paying attention and noticing where in your body you might be feeling tense, tight, sore, or uncomfortable. Simply notice these areas. You do not have to do anything about it, just notice. As you gently pay attention to your body and its different parts, remind yourself that you are lovingly interested in your body and your well-being. Now, allow this attention to move gently through your body.

Beginning with your head, noticing how it feels ... then moving down to your neck and shoulders ... paying attention to feelings and sensations ... tight or loose ... heavy or light ... now moving down through the back and spine and all the way down to the tailbone ... coming around to your belly ... paying attention to your abdominal area and noticing if there is tension ... moving toward your pelvis then down into your legs ... noticing any discomfort or tightness ... finally moving down to the feet and to the tips of the toes ... simply noticing and paying attention ... breathing deeply ... sending love, gratitude, and comfort to all the areas of your body ... reinhabiting and reacquainting yourself with your body.

Guided imagery and visualization

When we panic, our minds create images of dread and catastrophe. Our minds are powerful creators of pictures and visual representations of what we are feeling. When I am panicked, my mental imagery tends to turn bleak and foreboding, and I visualize things in tones of gray and muted colors. Our mind, with its creative prowess, also has the capacity to draw up imagery of lightness and comfort. The skill is to be able to tap into mindfulness to soothe ourselves with gently imagery and visuals during times of stress, overwhelm, and panic.

Start by thinking about the types of images that might help you and would provide a feeling of comfort during overwhelming moments. For me, these are often images of nature, some general and some more specific. When my mind can see an image of a peaceful, green field or meadow, it tends to experience a sense of calm. More specifically, I can call up a visual memory of my grandparents' property, which was peaceful, rural, and full of trees, flowers, and rolling green hills. These images work to reduce my more intense and foreboding panic-related mental imagery. Think about the types of imagery and visualizations that might help you during times of panic and overwhelm.

Images that might provide comfort and soothing when I am feeling panicked:

_____

_____

_____

_____

_____

The imagery that you listed above can be added to your coping toolbox, and you can access these soothing mental visuals when you are feeling panicky. When the mind feels soothed, the body follows suit. Gentle and comforting visualizations can work to reduce feelings of panic. Notice how, in the example below, the senses of sight, hearing, touch, and smell are also used to assist the body in calming and soothing itself. We can call up peaceful and soothing visualizations any time that we are feeling overwhelmed.

I am walking through a lush, green field. It is a warm and sunny day, and I can hear bees buzzing and birds chirping. The wind rustles gently through the leaves of the tall trees that surround the field. I can feel the soft grass beneath my feet and the clean, calm air smells comforting as I breathe it in. As I walk, I feel a sense of peace and tranquility.

Candle/object meditation

You may feel that meditation is easier if you have a focal point. You can pick something to focus your attention on and meditate with that particular object as your grounding point. A candle is a good option because, much like our thoughts, its flame flickers and moves, jumps and dances. As we meditate, we simply watch and pay attention. We notice the flame and use it as a point of focus without judging it, analyzing it, or drawing conclusions, as is always our intention when we practice mindfulness. As you observe your chosen object, remain:

- attentive
- non-judgmental
- focused
- calm.

You do not have to use a candle to do an object meditation. You can focus on a single point in a room, such as a corner, or object in the room, such as a painting or lamp; if you are outdoors, you can focus on a tree, a single branch or leaf of a tree, or even a cloud in the sky. As long as your intention is to pay nonjudgmental attention to your selected focal point, any object will work. Shifting the focus from inside of ourselves to external objects can gently pull us out of panic-driven thoughts.

Pebble/tactile meditation

Our sense of touch can help us in times of panic. Utilizing touch brings us back into our bodies and into the present moment. As we touch an object, our body and mind focus on the sensation of how it feels rather than on other mental stimuli and attachments. In the meditation below, we will use a pebble, but you can use any object that you can run your fingers along and that allows for the use of your sense of touch.

Begin by taking a deep and cleansing breath, inhaling through your nose and exhaling out of your mouth. Hold this pebble gentle in your fingers, noticing and paying attention to its surface and how it feels against your skin. Is it smooth or rough? Just pay attention … noticing how the pebble feels … welcoming and embracing the sensations on your skin, your fingertips … Gently focus your attention away from other concerns and onto the pebble that you hold in your hand … using your sense of touch to bring you back into the present moment.

Walking meditation

Meditation is not only performed in the "lotus" position; we can actually meditate even as we walk. Thích Nhất Hạnh, a Buddhist monk and teacher, describes it this way: "When you walk, arrive with every step. That is walking meditation. There is nothing else to it."[2] What he means is that, as we walk, we focus only on our footsteps; with each footstep, we arrive at a moment of grounding and solidity. We are present and attentive with each step we take.

So often, we walk unthinkingly and almost unconsciously. We rush to get to the next place, rarely paying attention to ourselves as we travel from point A to point B. Because panic thoughts are always rushed and chaotic, anything we can do in our daily lives to slow down and pay attention can work to reduce these fast-moving feelings and sensations. The next time you are walking, make a practice of paying attention to your body and to your feet as they touch the ground with each step you take.

Pet meditation

Panic and anxiety can have an isolating effect. Spending time with another living being can help us to feel alone with uncomfortable emotions and physical sensations. If you have a pet, you have a built-in resource for soothing yourself by connecting with another living thing. Animals have a natural ability to be mindful: they are often focused on whatever they are doing in the moment, with joyful and interested attention. We can take a lesson from our beloved animal friends to help us direct our attention away from rumination or anxious thoughts and towards the present moment.

First, become comfortable in a calm and quiet environment beside your pet. Take a few minutes to simply direct your attention toward this animal. You can pet, hold, or just observe them. As you do so, breathe naturally. Allow yourself to be fully present with this other living being. Embrace thoughts of wonder and respect toward this animal. Pay attention to your pet's features, such as their color, shape, and texture. Notice their breathing and their movements. Recognize your connection to this being and to everything in the world. Throughout this exercise, breathe deeply and naturally.

Acceptance

Mindfulness is a practice of acceptance. It encourages us to take a rational view of the present and to accept the current state of things. By doing this, we let go of harsh judgment of our feelings and of self-defeating thought and belief patterns. Viewing uncomfortable feelings as part of the experience of living can be helpful. Allow yourself to accept the following:

- I will always have thoughts, and they may not always be comfortable.
- I accept all of my thoughts and feelings without judging them as "good" or "bad," "right" or "wrong."
- I recognize that all thoughts and feelings are temporary and pass.
- I accept that feelings of worry and anxiety are commonly experienced.
- I accept that it is unreasonable for me to expect myself to never have an anxious or panicky thought.

Being gentle and patient with yourself

You might be thinking that I am able to implement these practices without fail whenever I need to. I have a confession to make: I sometimes struggle to implement these grounding and mindfulness strategies even though I am a therapist and I write the kinds of books you are reading right now. As we begin to implement new and helpful practices into our lives and to build our coping toolboxes, we need to practice self-compassion and gentleness. While we try our best to cope with discomfort, anxiety, and panic, it is not only OK but also normal to sometimes have difficulty implementing strategies. But every time you reach for a coping strategy when panic occurs, you can consider it a victory and a step closer to releasing panic's grip.

6

Cognitive behavioral strategies for panic

Though panic presents itself in our bodies, it begins in our thoughts. Our cognitions drive our physical responses, so one way we can control panic is by learning to question some of our thoughts rather than simply accepting them as factual. This is the aim of cognitive therapies such as cognitive behavioral therapy (CBT), dialectical behavioral therapy (DBT), and rational-emotive behavioral therapy (REBT). What all of these therapies have in common is that they teach us to investigate the connection between our thoughts and our behaviors. This chapter will draw on these therapeutic modalities to help you learn practical skills for challenging anxious and panic-driven cognitive patterns.

Seeing thoughts as fragments

We tend to assume that thoughts are fully formed, complete, and accurate conclusions. If, however, we begin to view thoughts as fragments, we alleviate the pressure to simply accept and act on them. When we really simplify panic, it is often a behavioral response to a thought. For example, a thought tells us "this is dangerous," and our body responds by pumping more cortisol, accelerating its heart rate, and tightening its muscles.

If we slow down this often immediate physical and behavioral response, we are less likely to slip into panic. We can do so by recognizing thoughts for what they really are: bits and pieces of our lives, experiences, observations, and memories. They can be random, unexpected, interrupting, and nonsensical. If we give our thoughts too much credence and credit, we are easily swept away in them and prone to overresponding—which often invites panic.

Building on the concepts and tenets of mindfulness, the first step in questioning our thoughts is to observe them. Take a moment to consider how many thoughts you have had today. If you tried to write down each one, your hand would ache and your pen might run out of ink. Anxiety and panic latch on to each thought rather than letting them simply come and pass. But this is precisely what they will do if we allow them to—come and pass, come and pass. In attempting to be less attached to each thought you have, begin to see them as clouds in the sky. No single cloud remains in the sky permanently, and neither does any single thought. Each makes way for another, then another, then another.

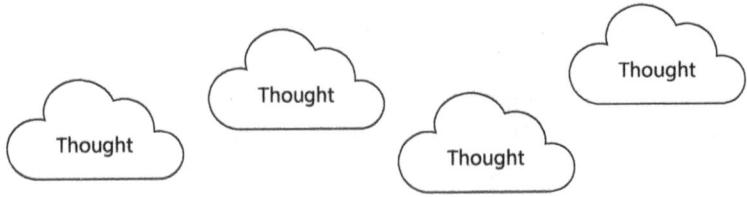

We get stuck when we believe each cloud requires an action. While it is true that some clouds may contain rain, thunder, or lightning—in which case moving indoors would be a helpful action—many clouds are simply there and don't require us to do anything at all. The same goes for thoughts: some require action and some do not. The skill is our ability to differentiate and to know when a behavioral response is required and when it is not.

Think for a moment about how many thoughts you have had today. Try to identify three of them. Record these thoughts below and note whether any behavioral response is required. Here is an example to get you started:

Thought: <u>It is not as sunny at the moment as it was a few hours ago.</u>
Behavior required: Yes   No

1 Thought: _____
Behavior required: Yes   No
2 Thought: _____
Behavior required: Yes   No
3 Thought: _____
Behavior required: Yes   No

Keep this analogy of thoughts being similar to clouds in your mind as you continue to build your skills for coping with panic. Every thought that pops into your head in the course of your day will also move on and make way for another thought. And not every thought will require you to do something.

Creating space between stimulus and response

If we accept that thoughts are as temporary as passing clouds, why then do we tend to react to each one as though it requires a response? The simple answer is that "doing something about it" is ingrained in us. We like to be able to act when a problem arises. Cognitive therapy encourages us to stop viewing every thought as a problem to be solved, and to investigate our thoughts with a rational eye. The skill in doing this is being able to create space in between the thought we have and the thing we tell ourselves we need to do about the thought.

Melanie

Melanie experienced severe illness anxiety. When her body would experience uncomfortable physical sensations, like a scratchy throat, a numb elbow, or a headache, her mind would take over and tell her to *do something* about them. This something was most often to seek immediate emergency medical care. Melanie spent a great deal of time in emergency rooms, urgent care centers, and doctor's offices. She would tirelessly research her physical symptoms online and look for something she could do to find an answer.

This is the definition of jumping from stimulus to thought to response.

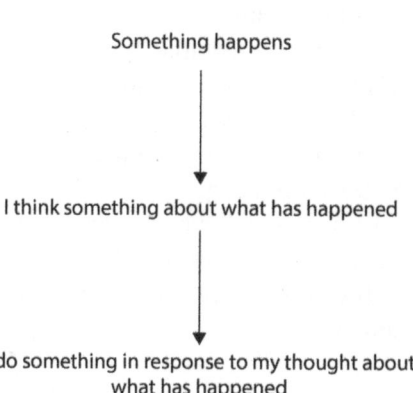

Something happens

I think something about what has happened

I do something in response to my thought about what has happened

Specifically, this equation might look like this for Melanie:

Stimulus: Severe headache
Thought: I am having some sort of medical emergency.
Response: I go to the emergency room.

The problem with Melanie's rush to response was that it actually escalated her anxiety, got in the way of her daily life, and made her perpetually on guard and hypervigilant. Notice that Melanie's response is not a response to the actual stimulus but, rather, to her thought *about* the stimulus. This is the place where we need to learn to pause before we respond behaviorally. Using the acronym SPACE, we aim to do the following:

Stop	Quite literally, stop yourself. Simply acknowledge that something is happening (stimulus) but don't rush to do something about it (response).
Pace yourself	Slow down. Breathe. When we panic, our thoughts move at lightning speed. Don't do anything in this moment.
Acknowledge	Recognize this thought's existence without latching on to it. Think about your thoughts as clouds that pass.
Calm/ground	Implement grounding techniques to help you soothe yourself.
Examine	View your thought rationally, making a concerted effort to avoid jumping to a panic-driven behavioral response.

A more measured, less anxiously responsive approach might look like this:

Stimulus: Severe headache
Thought: This is uncomfortable but it could be caused by many things and it is not necessarily a medical emergency.
SPACE: I take a deep breath. I acknowledge my thought about my headache. I implement my grounding techniques. I let go of the urge to "do something."
Response: I take a pain reliever. I take a break from my laptop and devices to let my eyes rest. I choose not to delve into internet research of my symptoms. I wait and see whether my symptoms improve.

When we learn to create space in between stimulus and response, we resist the urge to jump to an often panicky behavioral response. Notice the second example brings up more options, whereas in the first example, a jump is made immediately to an emergency response. Creating a space between the stimulus and the response allows us to slow down racing and catastrophic thoughts and to view the situation through a less anxious and panicky lens.

Below, you can track your own thought and behavioral process to help you begin utilizing the skill of creating space for yourself between stimulus and response:

Something happens:

_____

My thought about what happened:

_____

_____

SPACE (my use of stop, pace, acknowledge, calm, examine):

_____

_____

My behavioral response to my thought:

_____

_____

Automatic thoughts

The thoughts described above are defined in cognitive behavioral therapy as **automatic thoughts**. These types of thoughts are similar to psychical reflexes: they occur unconsciously, much like when a doctor strikes your knee with a reflex hammer and your leg automatically jumps. Unchallenged automatic thoughts can directly lead to panic. An automatic thought may look like this:

Person notices the faucet dripping

Automatic thought:
"The house will be flooded."

In this example, as is often the case with automatic thoughts, there is a catastrophic tone to the cognition. From there, the mind and body will respond to this catastrophic nature by emitting panic signals and initiating the snowball effect of panic. Automatic thoughts pave the way for panic.

Automatic thoughts are typically "if thoughts," cognitions about what might happen. Further, they often take on a tone and feeling of foreboding and of something bad bound to occur. The acronym **IF THOUGHT** will help you to begin questioning these automatic thoughts rather than simply accepting them as accurate:

Is my thought ...

Factual?	Is this thought grounded in facts or is it more based upon supposition, prediction, and assumptions?
Thorough?	Is this thought complete or is it more fragmentary? What does it ignore in terms of what is really happening?
Helpful?	Is this thought helpful to you or does it actually cause further distress, anxiety, and worry?
An Overresponse?	Is this thought a catastrophic response to something that is happening? In other words, do we see a dripping faucet and respond as though the house is under water?
Unreasonable?	Is this thought reasonable? Does it come with a realistic expectation of myself? For example, a leaky faucet that comes with the thought that you now need to sell your house and move is unreasonable.
Grounded?	Does this thought come up while you are in a grounded and rational state? Is this thought exacerbated by external influences such as fatigue or overwhelm?

Hurried?	Is this thought fast-moving and impulsive? Are you having this thought in a state of calm or in a state of escalation?
Triggered?	Is this thought the result of something that has happened in the past? For example, does this situation *feel* like a previous situation in which something negative occurred and is it driven by worry about reexperiencing the previous scenario?

When we ask ourselves these questions, we begin to take an investigative approach to our thoughts. This gentle yet curious investigation can help us to reduce the tendency to panic.

Use this investigative template to help you question rather than react to your automatic thoughts:

Is my thought ...

Factual?_____

Thorough?_____

Helpful?_____

an **Overresponse?** _____

Unreasonable? _____

Grounded? _____

Hurried? _____

Triggered? _____

Phil (author)

At times in my journey through panic, I have felt like a poster child for automatic thoughts. My type of automatic thoughts tend to take the form of catastrophic conclusions about my health. These thoughts leave little room for other interpretation or possibility.

This is the nature of automatic thoughts: they are rigid, inflexible, and often unhelpfully negative. If we look at these types of thoughts logically, we recognize that their rigidity directly leads to panic and overwhelm and can escalate to avoidance and panic attacks. For me, it typically looked like this:

>**Situation:** I feel an unexpected tightness in my chest.
>**Automatic thought:** I am having a heart attack.

As I learned the nature of these thoughts and began to understand that they were not only unhelpful but also inaccurate, they began to lose their power and I became able to explore other possibilities. Through a cognitive behavioral lens, I began to question the evidence—or lack thereof—behind my automatic thought. By adding cognitive questioning, I became able to work through my automatic thoughts, and reduce my anxious belief that they were facts. Cognitive questioning might look like this:

>**Situation:** I feel an unexpected tightness in my chest.
>**Emotions:** I feel afraid and worried.
>**Automatic thought:** I am having a heart attack.
>**Percentage belief in automatic thought:** 95%
>**Evidence to support automatic thought:** My chest feels tight. (Notice that this is the only "evidence" I really have—and it is not really evidence; it is a physical sensation.)
>**Alternate possibility:** I am experiencing a tight muscle in my chest area.
>**Reattribution:** I can attribute this thought to anxiety and not accept it as a fact.
>**De-catastrophizing:** I have no other physical symptoms aside from tightness, and there is no reason to believe that I am experiencing a heart attack.
>**Outcome:**[1] My belief in my automatic thought has decreased. My belief is now closer to 95 percent.

You can work this process by recording your automatic thoughts and implementing the questioning approach described above:

Date: _____

Situation: _____

Percentage belief in automatic thought: _____%

Emotions:

_____

Automatic thought(s):

_____

_____

Evidence:

_____

_____

Alternative possibility:

_____

_____

Reattribution:

_____

_____

De-catastrophizing:

_____

_____

Outcome:

_____

_____

New percentage belief in automatic thought: _____%

Cognitive distortions and incorrect meanings

It is human nature to derive meaning from things we think and experience. But, in terms of panic, this natural tendency can lead us to draw incorrect and frightening conclusions.

Gerald

Gerald, a 16-year-old high school student often derived meaning from the amount of time it would take a friend to respond to a text message. If, for example, his friend took an hour or two to respond, Gerald would interpret this as meaning that the relationship was in danger and that the friend no longer wanted to communicate with him. If, on the other hand, his friend responded immediately, Gerald felt safe and secure in the friendship. On both sides of the situation, Gerald added meaning: an immediate response meant strength and trust in the friendship, whereas a slow response meant the friendship was on rocky ground.

In an anxious and panicked state of mind, Gerald was unable to see any nuance in the situation. He could not recognize that the time between each text message did not necessarily mean something about the status of the relationship. Rational and comforting thoughts such as "Maybe my friend is busy or not near his phone" did not occur to Gerald in these moments, so obscured were they by his anxiety-driven conclusions.

Letting go of perceived meaning is a skill of cognitive behavioral therapy. The benefit is that it keeps our minds from running amok, ruminating, and fixating on a sense of danger, risk, and uncertainty, the places where panic thrives. If Gerald were to recognize that there are actually numerous possibilities of why a person might not respond to a text message, he might feel less panicky in response to the stimulus. Here is what this might look like from a cognitive behavioral perspective:

> **Situation:** My friend has not responded to my text message and it has been a few hours.
>
> **Thought:** This is taking longer than I wanted.
>
> **Anxiety-driven meaning:** My friend does not like me anymore.
>
> **Other possibilities:** My friend is busy. My friend has not yet seen my text message. My friend is not near his cell phone. My friend is in a place where he does not have cell service. My friend does not respond to text messages as quickly as I do. My friend does not know my expectations for how quickly text messages should be responded to.

Learning to allow for other possibilities beyond our anxious conclusion is a way to interrupt the thoughts that lead us down the road of panic. Here is a template you can use for beginning to explore other possibilities beyond the anxiety-driven conclusion:

Situation:

_____

Thought:

_____

Anxiety-driven meaning:

_____

_____

Other possibilities:

_____

_____

_____

_____

_____

Probability overestimation

Panic can take a "tunnel vision" form, ignoring various elements in favor of a single, negative element. When this occurs, we tend to overestimate the likelihood of something happening. Aaron T. Beck, originator of CBT, describes it this way: "The notion that it *could* happen carries almost as much weight as if it *did* happen." He goes on to describe these as "hypothetical infringements."[2] And these overestimations do just that: they infringe upon our lives and our ability to feel safe and protected.

In my own experience with illness anxiety, I would often see a common cold as possibly advancing to something more dire like pneumonia. I had no evidence of this occurring, but my anxious mind would quickly and easily overestimate the possibility and, in fact, confuse possibility with probability.

In another example, say you're driving as it begins to snow lightly. You immediately imagine the car careening off the road and crashing in a horrible weather-related accident. To take it a step further, in this example, there might even be no heavy snow or dangerous weather in the forecast and the car might be equipped with all-weather tires, yet your anxious mind might still draw a catastrophic conclusion.

In both examples, the mind attempts to do something it logically and scientifically cannot: predict the future. Our minds do this to keep us prepared and safe. But they simply cannot predict or prepare for every eventuality or outcome. This is the flaw in anxious and panicked thought processes. In altering these unhelpful thought patterns, we first need to pay attention to the difference between two easily confused words:

Possibility: *could*—but is not necessarily likely to—occur
Probability: *likely* to occur

Once we recognize this distinction, we can actively question whether our estimations are accurate or helpful. The following questions can help to investigate the conclusions we draw:

- Am I overestimating the possibility of this happening?
- Am I confusing possibility with probability?
- Am I trying to predict the future?
- Is my estimation coming from a place of logic or of anxiety?

Overgeneralization

When we overgeneralize, we look only at one or two pieces of information and ignore the many other pieces of information that might reduce our fear or panic. In essence, we unknowingly focus on evidence that supports the threat we feel rather than on evidence that goes against the perceived threat. It is as if we are working against ourselves like a prosecuting attorney trying to convince a jury. By highlighting only certain information and minimizing other information, the attorney sways the jury to vote a certain way for a desired result.

Daniel

Daniel experienced a panic attack prior to giving a presentation at his job. Though he was well prepared, he felt anxious and experienced feelings of dizziness and physical discomfort as it got closer and closer to the time to give his presentation. He was able to go through with his presentation, but the experience convinced him of a rigid "fact": any work presentation would result in panic. In overgeneralization, we take a single event and tell ourselves it represents an invariable rule.[3] For Daniel, this single event of feeling panicky before a work presentation meant that he would *always* feel panicky when preparing to present at work. This type of cognitive overgeneralization causes us to incorrectly assume future outcomes and ignores other positive elements of situations.

Consider Daniel's situation:

Highlighted information: "I panicked when I had to give a presentation."

Overgeneralized conclusion: "I will always be panicky when I have to give a work presentation."

Ignored information: "I was prepared for this presentation. I was nervous before but the presentation itself went very well. I had difficulty sleeping last night and that may have been part of why I felt panicky. Aside from this one occasion, I have never before experienced panic when preparing for a work presentation."

New conclusion: "What I experienced before this presentation was an outlier. There were other factors that may have contributed to feeling panicky and this does not mean that I will always feel this way before a presentation."

When it comes to coping with panic, what we ignore is as important as what we focus on. As you continue working to investigate your panic and anxiety-related thoughts, remember that there are often other parts of the situation that you may be minimizing but that are necessary in viewing things in a complete way. Ask yourself these questions before you draw an inflexible conclusion:

- Am I highlighting only one aspect of this situation?
- Is this singular attention causing me to draw an overgeneralized conclusion?
- What other information am I leaving out?
- By paying attention to these other aspects of the situation, how does my conclusion change?

Misattribution

Sometimes when we panic, we get the cause of our panic wrong. For example, if I panic while I am driving, I may incorrectly attribute my panic *to* driving, and conclude that driving is dangerous, risky, and should be avoided if I want to be safe and not feel panicked. This type of misattribution can lead us to avoidant behaviors and disrupt our lives. Panic is often a multidimensional response: it occurs for a variety of reasons. Fatigue, stress, burnout, and other contributing factors are often beneath our panic experiences. Misattribution is an under-recognition of other contributors and a simplistic and incorrect belief that the situation in which the panic occurred is the cause of the panic.

Francine
Francine experienced a panic attack while exercising at the gym. In that situation, she began to feel dizzy, short of breath, and overheated. She rushed out of the gym, fearful that she was going to faint. Though she enjoyed exercising and going to the gym, Francine began to feel panicky during future workouts. To Francine's anxious mind, the gym itself was the cause of her panic. This is the nature of anxious misattribution: it latches on to a single unpleasant experience and convinces us that whatever we were doing at that moment is the cause of our panic.

Viewing this situation differently, multiple factors might cause the feelings Francine experienced while working out, including dehydration, overexertion, muscle fatigue, and insufficient rest time between exercises. But to the anxious mind, the highway, the airplane, the shopping mall or, in Francine's case, the gym, is incorrectly interpreted as the cause of the panic. Once misattribution occurs, we can become unhealthily avoidant of the places where we experienced panic, viewing them as places of danger. Here is an example of how Francine can challenge her misattribution:

Location where panic was experienced: Gym
Misattribution: The gym is a place where I will always feel panicky.
Behavioral response: I should avoid the gym.
Other possible contributors: Dehydration, overexertion, fatigue

Reattribution: My panic may have been caused by other factors, not by the gym itself.

New behavioral response: The gym is a safe place but I need to make sure that I am hydrated and that I do not overdo it when I work out.

Just as Francine was able to do, you can begin to pay attention to occasions when you misattribute panic and use cognitive questioning to realign your behavioral response

Where I experienced panic:

_____

Misattribution of panic to specific location:

_____

Behavioral response:

_____

_____

Other possible contributors to panic experience:

_____

_____

_____

Reattribution:

_____

New behavioral response:

_____

_____

Anxious mind and rational mind

In the exercises presented thus far, there is a common theme: rational thinking can help us to limit the interference of panicked and catastrophic thoughts. In dialectical behavioral therapy (DBT), a distinction is made between the emotional mind and the rational mind. At the intersection of the two, we find our "wise mind." This is the place where we are not ruled only by emotion or only by logic. In a wise-minded state, we are less influenced by emotions and our responses are more measured and rational.[4] Because panic is an emotional experience, it can be difficult to tap into rational thinking when we are panicking. Finding a healthy crossover where we acknowledge our emotions but also do not allow them to take over is key in learning to cope with panic.

If we view our minds as being divided into these three parts—emotional, rational, and wise—we can work to train them to work together rather than against one another. Allowing for and accepting the coexistence of two seemingly incompatible feelings can help us to feel less rigid during times of panic. For example, I can feel afraid but also logical at the same time. I can be panicky but also capable simultaneously. Take a leap with me: I can *feel* unsafe but *be* safe at the same time. If I listen closely to my mind when I panic, I can distinctly see how my anxious mind and my rational mind respond. It may sound like this:

Anxious mind:

- "This is dangerous."
- "I need to get out of here."
- "Something bad is happening and I am at imminent risk."
- "I need to do *something* right now to keep myself safe."

Rational mind:

- "This only feels dangerous. It is not actually dangerous."
- "I do not need to flee this situation."
- "There is not an emergency occurring right now."
- "I do not necessarily need to do anything in this moment."

When I invite my wise mind into the equation, it works to create a comforting intersection where my experience is more balanced:

Wise mind:

- "My feeling of danger is just my anxiety. I am safe. I am OK."
- "It is normal to feel like leaving when I am panicky. But it is OK to stay here because I am safe."
- "Panic always feels like there is an emergency happening but it does not mean there actually is."
- "Because I know I am safe, all I really need to do right now is to try to calm and soothe myself. What do I need at this moment?"

Notice how the wise mind validates feelings but also speaks from a rational perspective, integrating the two to help us feel soothed and safe. We can tap into this wise voice at any time when we are feeling waves of panic. Think about what your anxious mind and your rational mind tend to tell you, then think about how your wise mind can work to integrate the two in a way that can offer you comfort:

My anxious mind:

_____

_____

_____

My rational mind:

_____

_____

_____

My wise mind:

_____

_____

_____

Distress tolerance

Another concept of DBT, distress tolerance is the idea that we can experience discomfort without it overtaking us, and we have the natural ability to tolerate uncomfortable feelings and situations. A simple way to look at it is as "riding a wave," rather than being pulled underwater by it. Distress tolerance also encourages us to accept that discomfort is a part of life and that we can never completely avoid it. When we are "distress intolerant," our bodies respond with anxiety and panic. When, on the other hand, we accept that distress will occur as a part of life and we give ourselves the credit to believe that we can withstand it, we are more readily able to access and utilize our coping skills and strategies. The following visualization will help you to understand the skill of distress tolerance:

Picture an ocean. Notice its waves as they roll in to shore, then retreat back out again. Recognize that the sea goes through both high and low tides. It is at times calm and tranquil and, at other times, more turbulent. Picture yourself on a raft on top of the ocean's surface. You are not thrown or tossed about by the ocean's movements; rather, you move along with the waves. They do not pull you under nor do they cause you to lose your balance. You skillfully navigate the changes in the ocean's movements.

The changes, transitions, and situations we encounter in our lives are similar to the currents and tides of the ocean; they vary in intensity and are never permanent. Although at times these changes in intensity can cause us to feel uncertain and panicky, we maintain the ability to navigate them. Take a moment to offer yourself the following affirmations to remind yourself of your ability to tolerate distress:

• I have experienced difficulties before and I have gotten through them.
• I trust myself to know how to navigate the challenges and uncertainties of life.

- I accept that it is not possible to live my life and never experience discomfort.
- I see myself as being able to "ride the waves."

"Shoulds," "musts," and "oughts"

Panic is heavily influenced by the rules we make for ourselves. Psychoanalyst Karen Horney wrote of what she termed the "tyranny of the should," and how our rigid and unforgiving adherence to these self-imposed "laws" often causes us to feel disappointment in ourselves. Horney viewed these as "inner dictates"[5] that might sound like:

- "I *should* never feel panicky."
- "I *must* be able to just get over this feeling."
- "I *ought* to not be so anxious."

Notice how unreasonable these inner laws are and how they can easily result in feelings of personal shortcoming and failure. At times when I have really struggled with panic, I have told myself the following:

- "I've got to get over this."
- "I need to stop being so anxious."
- "I shouldn't feel this way."
- "It is so ridiculous to be this panicky."

Challenging these inner dictates is part of panic recovery. Through my personal journey, these inner laws have changed significantly. Now, at a time when I am more accepting of and gentle with myself, they sound more like this:

- "I will sometimes feel anxious, even panicky, and that is OK. I know how to manage these feelings so that they do not take over."
- "I am actually not anxious or panicky all the time, just sometimes. So it is not helpful for me to make such rigid rules for myself."
- "Panic is not a ridiculous feeling—it is a frightening one. Telling myself it is ridiculous does not make me feel any better."
- "There is no 'right' way to feel when I am panicky. Telling myself there is a rule about this does not help me."

Think about your own inner dictates and how you might challenge them:

What "shoulds," "musts," and "oughts" do I tend to tell myself?

_____

_____

_____

Are these "inner laws" helpful to me?

_____

How might I challenge and change these expectations?

_____

_____

_____

Bringing it all together

The therapeutic strategies discussed in this chapter all have one thing in common: they encourage us to challenge our cognition. By doing so, we are able to change our behavioral response to panic and worry. Science shows that our neural pathways—the parts of our brains that hold thought patterns and behavioral habits—can be challenged, changed, and rerouted. Learning to question our automatic thought patterns can help us to loosen the grip of panic

7
More strategies for coping with panic

This chapter will discuss strategies that do not necessarily fit into the mindfulness or cognitive behavioral categories, but that can be helpful just the same. As your toolbox builds, you will feel more able to access what will help you in moments of panic.

Mantras

Mantras are short, simple, easily remembered statements that offer us soothing and comfort when we are overwhelmed and panicked. The language of panic is simplistic, telling us things like "This is bad," "You are in danger," and "The worst is happening." We can learn to meet these catastrophic statements with soothing statements of our own. When it comes to mantras, the simpler the better. Here are some of my mantras. Do not be deceived by their simplicity; it is precisely this simplicity that makes them effective:

- "I am OK."
- "I am safe."
- "This is a moment of discomfort."
- "I am calm."
- "I am not my anxiety."
- "This shall pass."
- "Breathe."
- "Slow down."
- "This feeling is temporary."

I have learned that these are the things I need to hear when I am struggling with panic.

Think about the things you need to hear, formulate them as simple mantras, and list them here:

_____

_____

_____

_____

_____

Affirmations

Similar to mantras, affirmations are self-statements that reassure and comfort us in times of overwhelm. While mantras are typically no longer than a few words and can be easily remembered and repeated, affirmations can be longer and take the form of positive statements that are directed at the self. Both serve to soothe the anxious, racing, and panicked mind. When we affirm our safety, competency, and ability to navigate difficult emotions, we build a feeling of self-trust that is often obscured during moments of panic. Affirmations that may be helpful during panic might sound like:

- "I am safe right now. My body knows just what to do to navigate these uncomfortable feelings. I trust my body to regulate itself."
- "Feelings of panic are temporary, and I know that what I am feeling right now will subside."
- "With each breath, I am grounding myself and returning myself to a state of equilibrium."
- "I trust myself to be able to navigate these feelings."
- "I am competent, capable, and resilient, and I know that I can cope with difficult situations and moments."
- "I acknowledge that I am feeling panic right now but I recognize that it will pass."
- "Even while this feeling is occurring, I am capable of creating an inner place of peace, tranquility and stillness for myself."

Think about what you need to hear during moments of panic and create some affirmations for yourself that you can use when you are feeling panicky:

_____

_____

_____

_____

_____

Soothing activities

Panic is a mental, physical, and emotional state of escalation. When we are escalated, we require calming and one of the ways we can reach a calmer state is by knowing and being able to access activities that allow us to slow down. Much like mantras, these activities are ideally simple and easily accessible. As you consider what types of activity might offer you soothing, think about how you are unique and tailor these activities to *you*. I, for example, am a person who enjoys nature, so I know that an outdoor-oriented activity will likely soothe me and help me feel less escalated. I am also a dog lover, so I know that doing something with my dog will likely help. I keep a mental list of my soothing activities that I can go to when I need them:

• Taking a short walk with my dog in a familiar area
• Sitting outside and just looking around
• Looking out of a window and paying attention to what I see
• Sitting quietly without noise or distraction.

These are the things that work for me. Notice how very simple they are and how they can be done without the need for travel or any apparatus.

Think about what types of activities would be soothing to you in
moments of escalation and list them here:

_____

_____

_____

_____

_____

Regression in service of the ego

Taking soothing activities a step further, the psychological concept of regression in service of the ego is about reengaging with
the types of activity that once awed us as children. While regression on its own is viewed as an unhelpful defense mechanism,
adaptive regression can be seen as helpful in restoring joy in our
lives.[1] When we see life through a carefree and joyful lens, feelings of dire seriousness and panic grip us less tightly.

At the age of 39, I took up model railroading. I had no experience with it and really no clue what I was doing. But, as I learned
the hobby, it became a source of joy and comfort. I would lose
myself for hours working on scenery and detail and creating my
own little world in miniature. Some might argue that this is a
somewhat juvenile hobby but, for me, it was and remains a coping mechanism in what can sometimes be a stressful and chaotic
life. In addition to model railroading, I also build Lego sets and
collect baseball cards. I do not see these activities as regressive
but, rather, as soothing, joyful, grounding, and healing.

A client shared with me that one day when she was stressed
she went out to her daughter's swing set on a whim and swung
back and forth for 15 minutes, feeling the breeze on her skin, and
contentedly engaging in this simple activity. She went on to share
that it made a significant difference in her day and her mood. She
felt that it had allowed her to step away from the busyness of life
for a short time and feel soothed and refreshed.

These types of seemingly childlike activity can serve to help us
navigate life with equilibrium.

What are some activities that might seem simple and even childlike but that you might consider trying or reengaging with to help you better manage stress, anxiety, and panic?

_____

_____

_____

Body-based strategies

In the example of the person who found comfort by swinging on a swing set, there was undoubtedly a physical release that occurred in addition to a mental and emotional soothing. Physical activity helps us to release cortisol and to redirect energy outward rather than inward, where it manifests as anxiety and panic. Strategies that focus on the body can help us to reduce pent-up cortisol and allow for relaxation rather than tension or tightening. Body-based coping strategies that might help you to reduce panic include:

- **Progressive muscle relaxation (PMR)**: This is an exercise in which we flex our muscles until we feel slight tension (for approximately 5 seconds), then release and allow ourselves to feel the muscles relax. Paying attention to the change between tension and relaxation can help to calm the body and nervous system. You can practice this with all of the muscular systems in your body.[2]
- **Yoga**: This ancient practice can help us to learn how to ground and calm our bodies. Yoga attends to both our musculoskeletal system and our respiratory system, helping us to reach a state of balance and equilibrium. Studies also show that a yoga practice can decrease anxiety and depression.[3]
- **Stretching**: When we panic, our bodies become "small," as we tighten up and restrict. Stretching can help us to expand ourselves physically, and to feel less constricted. This need not take the form of a full workout; a simple stretch of the arms upward will help you to ground and calm yourself.

- **Massage:** Panic and anxiety build up within our bodies, particularly in our tissues and muscles. Massage can help us to release built-up tension and restore a sense of calm and physical peace.

Imaginal exposure

We recognize how powerful the mind can be and how it can influence panic. But our imaginations can be used for positive outcomes just as much as they can frighten us or stress us out. In panic recovery, the mind needs to return to a state of feeling safe where it had previously felt in danger. Imaginal exposure is the concept of gently envisioning a return to the place or situation that we fear. We know we are safe because we are merely imagining this return. But, as the mind envisions and accepts the possibility of being able to face a feared stimulus, we begin to consciously accept the idea of returning ourselves to a situation that we have been avoiding out of fear.

When I experienced panic at the thought of walking my dog, I imagined walking him and everything going off without a hitch. I saw myself walking, my dog beside me, and nothing catastrophic happening. As I allowed myself to envision a safe and comfortable walk, I became more open to trying it once again. My mind began to become comfortable with the idea, and as I safely envisioned it more and more, I got to the point where I felt comfortable taking a walk with my dog.

Think about how imaginal exposure might help you in reengaging with an activity that you have avoided due to panic:

What scenario or situation would I like to be able to do once again?

_____

_____

What might envisioning myself doing this look like?

_____

_____

_____

_____

Speaking directly to panic

Panic and anxiety are storytellers: they make up narratives that cause us worry and dread. Their stories are often exaggerated, untrue, and narrowly focused on negative elements. We rarely challenge these stories. Instead, we accept them at face value and feel the intense emotions that come along with these narratives. Sometimes taking the power away from panic means speaking to it directly. In narrative therapy, the use of letter writing is a way to cultivate healing and to move away from a problem. Panic and anxiety often do most of the talking but, by writing a letter directly to them, we regain our voice and take back some of our power. This is an exercise I did years ago when I ran a narrative therapy group at an adolescent after-school program. Here is what I wrote:

Dear Panic,

I am writing to let you know that I am actively working to reduce your influence on my life. For a while, you made me feel as though I could not really be me or fully live. You caused me to doubt myself, feel unsafe, and avoid doing things that I enjoy. I want to tell you that I have decided to take my life back. I am learning how to cope with you, and I think you will notice that, lately, you have not been able to throw me off the way you once did. I am looking forward to continuing to move on from you. I will not miss you, and consider yourself on notice as you hear this letter.

Sincerely,

Phil

This letter is a direct address to a problem that had bothered me for a long time. I felt great healing and relief in putting my intention to move away from panic into words. I was taking back control and, as I wrote, panic seemed to get smaller and less threatening.

Write a letter to your panic in a direct and honest voice. Let it know how you feel and say what you need to say. As you write your letter, imagine panic growing smaller and less threatening:

Dear Panic,

_____

_____

_____

_____

_____

_____

_____

_____

Securing panic-related attachment

According to psychologist Abraham Maslow, once our basic physiological needs such as nutrition and safety are met, it is important that we fulfil the needs of love and belonging. Once we feel we belong and are loved, we can experience "self-actualization", a realizing of our full potential and capability.[4]

The experience I shared in Chapter 2 of moving into a new home by myself illustrates just how intense these isolation-driven feelings of perceived danger can be. My therapist at the time told me something very simple that has stuck with me all the years later: "Just because you are alone does not mean you are in danger." But panic doesn't always understand this rationale. Panic can mushroom out of feelings of being left out or ignored.

Feelings of isolation and rejection stem from our attachment style and whether it is secure or anxious. When we have a secure attachment style, we understand that a lack of physical presence does not necessarily mean we're being abandoned. For example, a young child with secure attachment to her caregiver understands that just because her mother is in a different room does not mean she has been abandoned. Anxious attachment is the very opposite: a confusion of distance with abandonment.

Research supports the idea that inconsistent relationships, particularly during childhood, can result in the development of panic disorder.[5] A parent who is unpredictable, behaves inconsistently, or is only intermittently present can instill lasting feelings of danger and worry in a child that can, later in life, result in anxiety and panic. When we work to heal our anxious attachment style, we reduce feelings of panic and worries that we will be abandoned. We can work to let go of our attachment-related fears by recognizing the following:

- Physical distance does not equate to threat or danger in a relationship.
- I can trust myself at times when I am alone. My safety does not rely on the presence of another person.
- I can communicate my feelings to my partner/significant other/family member/friend if I am feeling abandoned or unsafe.
- I can work through past situations, such as inconsistent parenting, that may influence my feelings of panic related to relationships.

Feeling your feelings

This may seem like a simplistic notion but allowing ourselves to experience our feelings is a radical act of coping with those uncomfortable, overwhelming, and frightening feelings. So often when we are emotionally uncomfortable, we tamp down or push away our feelings. While this can provide temporary relief, the feelings will eventually come out anyway, often in the form of anger, depression, anxiety, or panic. Accumulated emotion with no place to go will react like a tea kettle—once it can no longer sustain the heat, it will force a release. One way we can keep ourselves from reaching this "boiling point" is by actively working to acknowledge and "feel" our feelings so that they release and don't accumulate to an unhealthy degree.

Some ways we can "feel our feelings" are to:

- recognize that even uncomfortable feelings are allowable and acceptable
- keep in mind that, if we push away emotions, they do not resolve in a healthy way and will come out in unhealthy ways
- accept that responses like crying or feeling angry are normal human reactions and should not be viewed as weak or shameful
- recognize that it is normal to experience a wide range of emotions, both positive and negative.

What are some things you would like to keep in mind so that you allow yourself to feel your feelings?

_____

_____

_____

Making lifestyle changes

An immediately actionable strategy for reducing panic is to compassionately look at our lives and consider where we can make positive changes that might help us to improve our physical, emotional, and mental health. One way panic actually helped me is that I became a hydrator—I went from drinking barely any water over the course of a day to ensuring I stay hydrated. This might sound like a small thing, but it is exactly these small changes that can lead to reductions in panic and overwhelm.

Years ago, I had a panic attack and went to the emergency room. Once there, the doctor asked me, "What have you eaten today?"

I responded, "Nothing."

"What have you had to drink today?" he asked next.

"Coffee."

He nodded once. "Have you had any water?"

Sheepish now, I told him, "No."

You might be thinking, *Well, of course you had a panic attack if you were hungry, dehydrated, and hopped up on caffeine.* But this simply was not clear to me at the time—I had not yet made the connection between these simple daily habits and physical functioning. Now I recognize and preach the importance of staying hydrated and proper nutrition.

Think about the following areas of life and the listed guidelines and consider whether you would like to make any changes that might help to reduce panic:

Diet

Try to eat a well-balanced diet including:

- a variety of vegetables from all subgroups (dark-green, red, and orange, legumes, starchy, and other vegetables)
- fruits, especially whole fruits
- grains, at least half of which should be whole grains
- fat-free or low-fat dairy products
- a variety of high-protein foods such as seafood, nuts, lean meats and poultry, legumes, seeds, and beans
- oils (refined oils or oils high in saturated fat).

You should:

- limit saturated and trans fats, added sugars, and sodium[6]
- be mindful of alcohol, as it can exacerbate panic.

Hydration

- 72 ounces of water per day for women; 104 ounces for men.[7]

Caffeine

- No more than 400 milligrams (4–5 cups of coffee) per day.
- Wide variation between how individuals respond to caffeine intake.[8]

Physical activity

- Constant movement and ambulation throughout the day
- 150 to 300 minutes of moderate-intensity physical activity per week
- Muscle-strengthening activities of moderate or greater intensity at least two days a week[9]

Sleep hygiene

- Seven or more hours of sleep per night[10]

Based on the information and guidelines above, are there any areas of your life where you would like to make changes? If so, what are they and how do you plan to implement positive changes?

_____

_____

_____

_____

_____

Community and peer support

When we are struggling, there is strength in numbers. Knowing that we are not alone with our challenges can help us to cultivate a sense of community and healing. Seeking the shared support of others who face similar challenges is a positive and powerful action we can take for ourselves. This sense of community can begin at home when we allow ourselves to share our struggles with a trusted loved one or family member and can extend outward in locating support groups that focus on anxiety and panic.

Being open to the possibility of joining a community of others who understand what we are facing is an act of courage in your healing journey. Whether it is a virtual support group, an in-person group therapy setting, or simply an open conversation with a trusted person, connection is one of the ways we can cope with and heal from panic.

Part III
Overcoming panic

I openly and proudly describe myself as an anxiety and panic attack survivor. What I once viewed as a personal weakness and limitation, I now see as a point of resilience in my life. This recognition of ourselves as resilient and strong is an empowering component of healing from panic and letting go of the belief that it defines us. The final chapters of this book will focus on healing, resilience, and stepping back into our lives without panic at the controls.

8

Thriving in an anxious world

The idea that living in this world naturally comes with anxiety is not new. Ask anyone at any time in history, and they would likely say that the world is in some state of chaos and uncertainty. While we cannot always change the larger state of things, we can learn to care for ourselves, navigate our lives, and thrive despite the uncertainty of the world in which we live.

Resilience and self-efficacy

Start to feel safe and secure by reframing how you view yourself. Panic can become a self-fulfilling prophecy: the more we feel we are unsafe and at the mercy of our anxiety, the more we begin to believe it. Self-efficacy, a concept created by psychologist Albert Bandura, speaks of our innate ability to be competent and capable in our lives. When we see ourselves in this light, our self-image moves away from feeling incompetent and incapable. Below are three of the competencies of self-efficacy that you can continue to remind yourself of as you build and strengthen your panic-navigation skills:

Skills of self-efficacy

Self-awareness

- The ability to pay attention to and acknowledge our thoughts, emotions, and behaviors.
- In terms of coping with panic, being attentive to our thoughts can help us recognize how they affect our emotions and, in turn, our behaviors.

Self-regulation

- The ability to change our behaviors in order to better serve us and our desired outcome.
- When we manage panic, part of the goal is to be able to challenge and alter unhelpful behavioral responses.

Mental agility

- The ability to view a situation from multiple perspectives.
- Coping with panic requires us to see situations from various angles in order to differentiate between perceived danger and actual danger. A flexible rather than a rigid mind allows us to do this.[1]

Viewing ourselves as competent and resilient can feel strange and uncomfortable. It can be hard to take a compliment, especially from ourselves. But a positive self-view goes a long way toward not only feeling—but believing—that we can be OK in a world that is complex, complicated, and sometimes overwhelming.

Embracing the complexities of human existence

In order to fully view ourselves as competent travelers through our world, it is helpful to recognize that life and human existence are rarely simple. When we tell ourselves we should never feel worried or anxious, we invalidate the human experience. In making a conscious effort to accept life's complexities rather than to deny them, we reduce the self-imposed pressure to never worry as well as the guilt that we feel when we do worry.

With gentle acceptance, consider the following universal truths about life. Allow yourself to accept each one, knowing that acceptance is a part of coping and healing.

I accept that life is:

- challenging
- changeable
- complex
- multidimensional
- not easily defined
- nuanced
- uncertain
- unpredictable

Despite these truths, we live rich and beautiful lives. We navigate through life's uncertainties and emerge from many different challenges and difficulties. Take a moment to sit with this verse from the poet William Blake:

It is right it should be so;
Man was made for Joy & Woe;
And when this we rightly know,
Thro' the World we safely go.

William Blake, 'Auguries of Innocence'[2]

Moving through a complex world safely is our goal in panic recovery. Blake's advice, though almost two and a half centuries old, holds true today: accepting challenge just as easily and readily as we accept joy is vital to our ability to thrive and to live our lives to their full potential and capacity.

Normalizing worry

If we accept life is complicated, this allows us to normalize some of the uncomfortable feelings we experience in response to this complexity. Society often pathologizes and medicalizes commonly experienced human emotions, labeling them "disorders" or assigning psychiatric labels. While this can help us to understand and categorize symptoms, it can be detrimental to our feeling of "normalcy." We feel isolated and believe we are somehow broken compared to everyone else. When we work to normalize these feelings, we begin to view ourselves as acceptable:

- All people, no matter their status or station in life, experience worry and anxiety.
- Fear is a primal human emotion. The experience of fear does not indicate a psychological deficit or problem.
- Desiring safety is a normal human need, both physically and psychologically.
- Every human being's body contains a nervous system which can become activated by frightening or overwhelming stimulus.

Commonality can help cultivate healing from panic. Add the following affirmations to those you listed and created in the previous chapter in order to help you keep this commonality in mind:

- I am in no way broken or "less than" if I experience panic.
- Many people experience anxiety, panic, and panic attacks.
- Our world is complicated and it is OK to feel overwhelmed by it at some moments.
- It is normal to seek safety and to want to feel protected and secure.

Accepting existential anxiety

Many clients have told me, "I'm going through an existential crisis."

I always respond to this statement in the same way: "You are thinking existentially, and that is not a crisis." When we think existentially, we ponder profound and often unanswerable questions. Doing this is a healthy way to accept and embrace the uncertainties and complexities of life. Some common existential concerns include:

- What is the meaning of life?
- What is my purpose?
- What happens when we die?
- Is there an afterlife or eternal reward?
- What is the difference between "right" and "wrong"?
- What is love?
- Do we have free will?
- Is life predetermined?
- Is there true equality or justice in the world?

If we view these questions as unacceptable or verboten, they seem risky or dangerous. If, on the other hand, we view them as normal and commonly pondered, we feel less uncomfortable with them. The normalization of profound and difficult questions can provide us with a sense of peace in the midst of a world and a life that is full of unknowns. Because panic is often centered on control, an acceptance that we actually cannot control everything in our lives can bring comfort and healing. Psychologist Irvin Yalom argues that anxiety can be reduced to comfortable levels and used to increase our awareness and vitality.[3] Think of it this way: if I accept, for instance, that thoughts about death are not inherently risky, my anxiety about them decreases and my willingness to think about the topic intellectually and curiously increases.

Boundaries and compartmentalization in a complex world

Keeping ourselves psychologically safe means that we need to be mindful of just how much stimulus there is in our everyday lives. We are constantly inundated with external stimuli in the form of media, and it is a fine line between managing this constant stream and experiencing overwhelm and panic due to it. We tend to think of the concept of boundary-setting only in terms of personal relationships, but the need for boundaries extends beyond just interpersonal situations. If I watched a 24-hour news channel all day long, I might be bound to feel overwhelmed, vicariously traumatized, and panicky. So, it is vital to create healthy separation from these forms of constant information. We can do this by being aware of our level of exposure to the following:

- **News and media outlets**: I noticed recently while watching the evening news that, for 29 minutes, the programming was dedicated to unpleasant, traumatic, violent and sad stories. The final minute of the broadcast was reserved for an uplifting story. The nature of the news cycle is to focus on stories of tragedy and, in recent years, has grown to often include violent images and videos to accompany these stories. If we overexpose ourselves to these types of news stories, we risk causing ourselves anxiety and panic. We can become vicariously traumatized by viewing constant stories of disaster and tragedy. Be aware, too, that the nature of social media algorithms is to show you more of the same things you've viewed before, so one traumatic news story can beget others. It's important to set boundaries with social media to avoid this vicious cycle.
- **Triggering content**: From police "dashcam" videos to amateur disaster footage captured on cell phones, we are able to visually experience what is happening in the world in a way that

was once impossible. The problem with this accessibility is that it leaves us vulnerable to seeing images and unfolding events that we may not otherwise choose to view. Understanding what triggers us can help us make an informed decision regarding what we choose to view.

We must make a clear distinction between setting boundaries and being avoidant. Many of us believe that it is part of our social duty to know what is happening in our country and in the world. This means being able to control intake of information rather than to simply cease taking in information.

Boundary	Avoidant response
Limiting exposure to the news cycle and recognizing when you have reached a point of saturation.	Never watching the news or being willfully ignorant to what is happening in the world.
Allowing for time to "unplug" from devices in order to engage in other activities.	Being unhealthily averse to these forms of technology and, in turn, limiting ourselves from benefitting from their positive aspects.
A willingness to be selective and discriminating in what we watch, listen to, and engage with.	An all-or-nothing response in which we choose not to engage with any media, even that which is healthy and helpful.
Creating a balance of informative/ news-oriented information and entertainment/enjoyable programming.	Engaging in *only* one form of media or forgoing *all* forms of media.

In addition to boundary setting, compartmentalizing—our ability to "put things on a shelf" so that we can go back to them at a later and better time—is a skill for managing the influx of stimulus in a complex world. As I write this book, there is a violent conflict in the Gaza Strip—it is all over the news and social media. As a social worker and human being, I know that it's important for me to understand what is happening in this part of the world, but I can only devote myself to this when I am reasonably able. I happened to see an upsetting social media news post about this conflict in between clients and had to choose to "put it on the shelf" for later. I recognized that it was a newsworthy story, but also that I simply did not have the time to devote to it at that moment. Compartmentalization helps us maintain balance and keeps us psychologically healthy.

We always have the ability to "shelve" things if we are too overwhelmed to attend to them in the moment. This extends far beyond just our relationship with media. In terms of how we cope with panic, compartmentalization is a healthier option than avoidance or suppression. It allows us the opportunity to come back to something when we are in a more balanced state. It has been stressed in this book that overwhelm can lead to panic, so our ability to simplify things for ourselves and prioritize what can reasonably deal with in the moment is vital. The "shelf" does not indicate that something is unimportant but, rather, that it requires a calmer time in which to be fully attended to.

In relation to this idea of putting things on a shelf in order to be able to devote proper time and attention to them, think about what is happening right now in your life that you might consider "shelving" for the moment so that you feel less overwhelmed:

_____

_____

_____

Staying true to your values

While we can work to control elements of our environment as discussed above, sometimes we need to consider the environment itself and how it may be contributing to our panic. When we force ourselves to remain in environments that are not healthy for us, we often experience extreme discomfort and panic. Ensuring that our jobs and relationships align with our personal value systems can help us to be in environments that suit us and that do not bring on anxiety or panic.

Rachel

Rachel had worked in finance for the past five years. But as time went on, she felt less and less that this world represented her or her personal values. The fast-paced and stressful nature of the finance field left her exhausted, burned-out, and feeling panicky. She often worked 12-hour days, was required to be available after work hours, and had little time to attend to other areas of her life. Rachel began to experience frequent panic attacks and came to dread going to work each morning. Though this was uncomfortable, it helped inspire Rachel to make an honest assessment of her satisfaction with her career.

Ultimately, she made a thoughtful decision to leave the finance field. She went back to school for elementary education and became a kindergarten teacher. In this job, she felt more aligned with her personal values. As she settled into a better role for herself, Rachel's feelings of panic and burnout dissipated.

Much as Rachel was able to do, if you feel like a specific environment or situation is contributing to your panic, ask yourself:

- Am I in a place where I can thrive?
- Are the environmental conditions right for me?
- Does this situation/environment/relationship align with my personal values?
- Might it be helpful to me to consider a change in environment/situation?

A plant or flower in the wrong environment cannot thrive and will be vulnerable to injury. The same goes for humans. When we are in invalidating or harsh environments, we bear the psychological injuries of stress, anxiety, and panic. Removing ourselves from environments that are not right for us is not an act of giving up—it is a mark of authenticity and courage. It helps us regain a sense of safety and allows us to feel secure in our surroundings.

Being sensitive in an insensitive world

Those of us who have a sensitive nature (I am in this category) are likely to feel things at a deep level. This, in turn, can mean that our anxiety strikes harder for us than it does for others. We may panic when others do not or become anxious faster than others do. This is not a sign of weakness; rather, it simply means that we have a higher sensitivity level. It also means that we need to recognize this fact about ourselves and take measures to ensure that we do not quickly slide into burnout and panic.

As a sensitive person and also a therapist, I absorb a great deal of emotion during the course of a day. My clients share difficult information, experiences, and feelings with me and I take seriously my vow to keep their stories safe and confidential. In essence, I have a lot of "stuff" that I carry around with me. It took me years to learn that this also means I have an upper limit of what I can healthily absorb. I had to find a way that I could be my sensitive self but also not overextend myself. Over time, I was able to work out a schedule that works for me and that honors the sensitive person I am. I see a maximum of 25 clients per week and no more than seven in one day—it took me a while to figure out that this was my limit. I try to give myself an hour break around midday and to not see clients after a certain time in the evening. When I get home, I never, ever read about or research psychology or mental health—I can't. My cup is already filled to the brim by that time.

Staying true to these guidelines for myself is not always easy. Society sends us a lot of unhelpful messages about work and productivity. Early in my career, I routinely overscheduled myself, worked later that I really wanted to, had poor boundaries with client communication, and took cases that, in retrospect, we not right for me. I constantly felt exhausted, I fretted about my clinical skills and effectiveness, and often experienced work-related panic. I was doing what I thought I was "supposed to" as a therapist— taking every case that came my way and trying to help everyone all the time. I know a therapist who sees double the number of clients in a week as I do. That might be right for them but it does not work for me. I am glad I have figured this out. If I hadn't, it is more than likely that I would not have lasted in this field. I would have burned out quickly.

Think about the person you are. Are you, like me, sensitive? Do you feel things deeply? Does too much emotion or exposure to others' emotions cause you overwhelm? What do you need to remember about yourself to help you maintain a balance that is right for you?

_____

_____

_____

_____

_____

How will you recognize when you are taking on too much, stretching yourself too thin, or not maintaining balance?

_____

_____

What will you do when you make this recognition?

_____

_____

Leaning into our sensitivity rather than being ashamed of it is a way for us to know how much stimulus we can handle. I have learned to view my sensitivity as a strength rather than as a weakness and that has been instrumental in my panic recovery. Sensitivity ended up being a tool for coping with panic that I did not even realize I had. Being sensitive allows me to:

- be acutely aware of how I am feeling and of my emotional state
- understand that my body, when feeling panicky, is trying to communicate something to me (very often, my body is trying to tell me to slow down or rest)
- recognize almost immediately what environments and situations are not right for me
- identify the sources of my panic
- treat myself compassionately when I am panicky and overwhelmed.

Finding peace in chaos

Our ultimate goal is to maintain inner peace and calm even if the world around us is chaotic and turbulent. In seeking this peaceful space, keep the following in mind, with the acronym **PEACE** to guide you:

- Personal values can guide your decision about which environments are right for you and which environments cause you discomfort, anxiety, and panic.
- Embrace the complexities of human life and recognize that all people experience challenges related to this complexity.
- Accept the world as being chaotic without having to be chaotic yourself.
- Compartmentalize and create boundaries for yourself with triggering or overwhelming stimulus; "shelve" things that you cannot realistically deal with in the moment in order to avoid overwhelm and panic.
- Existential thinking is a common human response and these types of thoughts and feelings can be welcomed rather than avoided or suppressed. By welcoming them, we take away their power to frighten and overwhelm us.

Peace can exist even during a storm. As you recover from panic, imagine yourself safe and secure even though there may be a strong wind or rainstorm. Living in a world of uncertainty requires us to be able to access inner peace and a still point where we are balanced despite external conditions. The meditation below will help you to remember that you have the ability to maintain peace, calm, and equilibrium even in the midst of a complex existence:

Begin by sitting comfortably and taking a few deep breaths, breathing in through your nose and exhaling through your mouth. With each breath, envision the word "peace." In and out ... peace. In and out ... peace. In and out ... peace. Now, as you continue breathing this way close your eyes and imagine yourself as a tree: you are tall and sturdy. Your roots reach far down into the earth. These roots are your personal values. They are everything you hold dear and true about life. They provide you with the foundation that keeps you upright and sturdy. Feel your strong roots fastened firmly to the ground ...

Now, imagine the sky and the atmosphere that surrounds you: at times, all is tranquil and calm; at other times, turbulent and stormy. No matter what the conditions, you remain firm, strong, sturdy, and tall. This is your ability to acknowledge and embrace all of the different conditions that may arise. You simply observe and acknowledge them from your rooted perspective. You neither blow over because of the wind nor burn because of the sun: you are simply present along with them. Notice the other trees, flowers, bushes, and plants around you. They, too, experience the changing and varying conditions. This is your ability to recognize that other beings beside yourself are aware of the world's complexity ...

Continuing to breathe in and out ... in and out, imagine a rainstorm arriving then passing. After it passes, the sun appears. After a time, the sun makes way for the gloaming of the evening and then the darkness of the night. This is you recognizing your ability to compartmentalize different parts of life and remembering that no state or condition is permanent. Finally, imagine your leaves beginning to change from summer greens to autumn yellows and oranges. You gently recognize that your life is impermanent yet you feel safe. This is you welcoming life's unanswerable questions ...

In the midst of changing conditions, weather, and external factors, you remain sturdy and tall. You are rooted and safe. Repeat to yourself, "I am peaceful and safe, I am peaceful and safe." Stay in this peaceful and safe mindset for as long as you wish. And, when you are ready, open your eyes and return to the present moment.

9

Feeling safe again

Panic and panic attacks take away our sense of safety. They cause us to feel persistently uneasy and vigilant. We step out of our lives when we are overcome with panic, solely focused on dealing with the present panic and preparing to deal with future panic. We have little time for our lives when we are stuck in this exhausting survival mode. Panic recovery, more than anything else, is a return to a sense of safety across our lives. We pick up activities that we had let go of, we refocus our priorities, and we no longer tiptoe through our lives, worried that we must dodge impending disaster. Our lives, which had become narrowed and constricted, open up once again.

Triage to maintenance

Before I learned to manage my panic, it drove me to doctors' offices, urgent care clinics, and emergency rooms on a regular basis. Panic convinced me time and again that I needed urgent medical attention. I spent a great deal of time and money seeking comfort and looking for assurance that I was healthy. This focus distracted me from my actual life, my job, my personal relationships, and my hobbies and interests. I was constantly attempting to triage a perceived situation of danger. Now, unless I have a physical injury or am clearly sick with a cold or flu, I visit the doctor once a year.

My panic recovery required a shift from triage to maintenance. By moving from hypervigilance to attention, I could feel safe and feel that I was living once again. Before, I was treadmilling, fixating, and ruminating. After, I was living in the moment and paying healthy attention to different parts of my life. For me, this pivot from hypervigilance to healthy attention looked like this:

Hypervigilance	Attention
Constant checking, assessing, and anxious fixation on my body/health	Healthy attention to my body that is not constant or anxiety-driven
Constant seeking of medical care and reassurance	Appropriate medical maintenance, resisting anxious urges to seek immediate care
Contingency planning and playing out possible future scenarios	Accepting that I cannot predict future scenarios and focusing on the "now"

This shift can create space in your life, allow you to breathe, and make room for those parts of your life that have become secondary in the face of constant panic. Hypervigilance obscures everything else, whereas attention simply means being aware without fixation, constant surveillance, or need for immediate action. Accepting that life is not a situation that requires constant triage can help you to let go of anxious habits and thought patterns.

Think about areas of your life in which hypervigilance has taken over and consider how to shift these areas to a more attentive approach:

Areas where I am hypervigilant	What healthy attention might look like

Chasing ghosts

As I recovered from panic, I needed to recognize that I was often "chasing a ghost," looking for a definitive answer to a vague concern or fear. Because panic often comes with a feeling that "*something* bad could happen," it was difficult to find a specific answer that would completely reassure me. When doctors assured me that I was healthy, it ironically served only to heighten my anxiety and panic—the lack of a specific answer kept the wheel of worry spinning and left me to think, rethink, and overthink.

Ultimately, therapy and education provided the answer I had been seeking. As I understood what anxiety and panic were, I began to feel a sense of relief and a willingness to reduce my fixation on chasing a specific, concrete answer.

Safety and reassurance can only come when we stop chasing reassurance and become OK with a little uncertainty. In a Buddhist tale, a man runs tirelessly, attempting to catch his shadow. Eventually, he dies of exhaustion never having realized that, if he had only stopped to rest, his shadow would have passed. We will not die of panic, but we can, if unchecked, lose important parts of our lives and ourselves through our constant searching and running.

Mourning the hypervigilant self

That time in my life spent chasing and reassurance-seeking was uncomfortable, but I do not shame myself for having experienced it. I know and accept that there were reasons behind this behavior, and that it was not, and is not, a sign of brokenness or weakness. We can look at part of our panic recovery as remembrance and mourning. Anytime we let go of something or lose something that has been in place for some time, we need to grieve the loss. It is a way for us to process our complicated feelings about what is no longer in our lives.

It may sound silly—why should we grieve something that we did not like and that only caused us discomfort? Sigmund Freud wrote that trauma—for our purposes, panic—"must no longer seem ... contemptible," but, rather, be viewed as something that existed for a reason and "out of which things of value for [the person's] future life have to be derived."[1] In other words, by viewing what we have been through without anger or contempt, we allow for it to carry meaning and to open the door to positive change.

By remembering what I will call "anxious me," I can let go of and move past that time in my life. I am able to view "anxious me" with compassion and to recognize that he felt unsafe and overwhelmed. In my grieving process, I can remember how:

- I lovingly and compassionately let go of anxious me
- I am grateful to anxious me for attempting to keep me safe but recognize I no longer need this part of myself
- I allow my feelings about this loss—whatever these feelings may be, they are all acceptable and I allow myself to experience them
- I let go of anxious me without feeling ashamed of myself or judging myself for having been worried and panicked
- I recognize that anxious me was a temporary version of myself.

Being reasonable with ourselves

As we grieve and move forward, we need to always do so with self-compassion. Moving into a less panicked state requires that we remain gentle and reasonable with ourselves. Though I am undoubtedly less controlled by panic than I once was, I still experience it at times. In some moments of overwhelm, those old feelings, symptoms, and sensations reappear. This in no way means that I am backsliding, regressing, or that my panic recovery was a fluke. I am not back to "square one" if I feel panicky. In fact, I am fully equipped to cope with these feelings in a way that, years ago, I wasn't. These feelings, while still uncomfortable, will not rule the day as they once did. Staying reasonable with ourselves can help us navigate our recovery from panic. These are reminders that I carry with me:

- I will still sometimes experience feelings of panic.
- I may have a panicky day sometimes.
- I may sometimes have difficulty accessing and implementing my coping skills and tools.
- I may sometimes experience frustration when I feel panicky.
- I will never completely eradicate all feelings of anxiety or worry.
- I accept that, although panic may still arise at times, I am equipped to cope with it in a healthy way and I remember that I possess the tools to navigate these feelings.

When we are unreasonable with ourselves and our expectations of ourselves, we often feel angry, disappointed, and ashamed. None of these self-imposed judgments are helpful in soothing ourselves when we are panicky. In those moments of emotional escalation and panic, it is more helpful to remember:

- I know what this feeling is and I know how to manage it.
- I know that this feeling of panic is temporary and will pass.
- I have experienced this type of feeling before and I have been OK.
- I have worked to build the skills I need to cope with this feeling.
- I am not doing anything wrong or "failing" because I am feeling panicky.

Dealing with a "flare-up"

Sometimes my panic flares up. I describe it this way so that I keep myself from viewing the return of a panicked feeling as a regression or a return to a previous state. Rather, I view it as a temporary agitation, much like feeling a muscle that was pulled weeks ago tinge even though it has recovered. This feeling of discomfort does not signify a reinjury or a new injury.

Panic can be viewed similarly: it will sometimes flare up or be stirred up again. When this occurs, remember that you now have a psychological understanding of panic, so it no longer presents itself as a vague and impossible-to-understand sensation. You can deal with the flare-up by building on this understanding of panic and taking a rational view of what you are experiencing.

The following questions can help you to cope with a panic flare-up without escalating your discomfort:

- **What are possible triggers/causes?** Think about what is happening in your life right now. Are you overwhelmed, busy at work, not feeling well, tired, or coping with other life situations? These can all impact the return of panic feelings. Understanding what may be underlying the flare-up is helpful as is not rushing to the conclusion that something catastrophic is happening.

- **How is my body responding?** Pay attention to how your body is responding to your panic feelings. It is likely responding in a predictable way, perhaps in your heart, respiratory system, gastrointestinal tract, or your head.

   When I have a flare-up, I immediately feel it in my chest. This is my common area for panic to manifest. It helps me to recognize that this feeling is not new and, therefore, I can confidently attribute it to a flare-up and not to something more troubling.

- **What tools can I use?** Think about what tools for coping with panic you can access and use in this moment. Which ones do you feel will be most helpful right now? Remember that you possess a wealth of coping tools, self-care plans, grounding techniques, and cognitive behavioral strategies to choose from. You know how to use each one in the most helpful way.

- **What do I need?** With a self-compassionate approach, ask yourself what you need right now during this flare-up. I, for example, often need to temporarily stop what I am doing. This helps me to ground myself and come back to a state of equilibrium. What do you need in a moment when panic is flaring up?

- **What do I need to remind myself?** What mantras, statements, or affirmations will offer you soothing in this moment? Remember that your self-talk is always a component of coping with panic. I often need to remind myself that "I am safe." What self-statements help you during these moments?

Below, create your own flare-up plan to help you feel that you can easily access your tools at moments when you recognize that you are experiencing panic. Most importantly, remember that a "flare-up" is *not* a regression or a failure.

Possible triggers/causes:

_____

_____

_____

How my body is responding:

_____

_____

_____

What tools I can use:

_____

_____

_____

What I need:

_____

_____

_____

What I need to remind myself:

_____

_____

_____

Giving ourselves credit

As a therapist, I often hear clients' stories and am struck by their strength and resilience. I make a point to let them know how strong they are, how inspiring their story is, and how important it is for them to also see themselves this way. This type of self-compliment is not always easy; we are often much quicker to self-judge and self-recriminate than we are to celebrate ourselves. But an important part of panic recovery is our willingness to celebrate our victories, give ourselves credit, and feel proud of our progress. I mentioned viewing myself as a "panic survivor," and I wholeheartedly see myself this way. I lived through the struggle and constant discomfort that comes with panic, and I came out the other side stronger and more resilient. Take a moment to give yourself credit for your progress:

- I am resilient, strong, and adaptable.
- I continue to learn how to manage panic and to reduce its impact on my life.
- I see my progress as something to be proud of and I celebrate myself through this journey.
- I give myself credit for the work I am doing to cope with panic.

What else would you like to say about yourself?

_____

_____

_____

Restoration of safety

In *Trauma and Recovery*, Judith Herman describes successful recovery as "a gradual shift from unpredictable danger to reliable safety ... and from stigmatized isolation to restored social connections."[2] Accepting that we are, indeed, safe underlies everything that follows in our recovery from panic. Our first step is to wholeheartedly believe that we are safe and not in imminent danger. We can remind ourselves:

- I am not in any type of clear and present danger.
- I am safe, secure, and protected.
- This moment is completely safe and without threat or risk.
- There is no disaster or catastrophe waiting to occur.
- I am equipped to handle any situation that might arise.

When we once again feel reliably and consistently safe, we reengage with our lives and we experience a sense of restoration. First and foremost, our daily functioning and activities of daily living are restored. This can look like:

- a reprioritization of daily tasks
- a renewed interest in activities that we had deprioritized or let go of due to panic
- a healthy and balanced integration of various components of our lives, including family, relationships, work, hobbies, and self-care
- attention to our physical well-being, daily self-care, and hygiene.

With our daily lives back in more stable condition, we move from constriction to expansion. Areas of our lives that had been narrowed by panic now expand, allowing for inclusion of all that is important and meaningful to us. It feels like stretching our bodies after a long period of being in an uncomfortable position. We go from being fragmented by panic and worry to being whole and feeling secure.

Reconnecting with our lives

When we overcome panic, it is as though we find our lives once again. As I recovered, I was able to reconnect with my devotion to and interest my work, my love for my family, and my personal interests and hobbies.

What are the areas of your life that you can now reconnect with or that you wish to reconnect with?

_____

_____

_____

Your recovery from panic allows you to have space for everything. Imagine a room cluttered with stuff: there is no room for anything else. This is similar to the panicking, fixating, and ruminating mind. Every nook and cranny is stuffed with thoughts, worries, fixations, conclusions, predictions, and contingency plans. Now picture this room uncluttered with open space for whatever you would like to put there. With panic out of the equation, we gain significant square footage in which to live our lives. Think about what you would like to put in this room. Whether it is time with family, time to rest, or time for pleasure, there is room for it all.

As you continue to move confidently through your panic recovery, keep the following in mind:

- I have power and autonomy in my life.
- Panic does not define me.
- Panic does not dictate my life and how I live it.
- Panic is a temporary feeling that has no power of permanence.
- I am here in my body. I am safe. I am secure. I am protected.

Notes

Chapter 1

1 Reprinted with permission from the *Diagnostic and Statistical Manual of Mental Disorders*, Fifth Edition, Text Revision (Copyright © 2022). American Psychiatric Association. All Rights Reserved.
2 Sansone, R. A., & Sansone, L. A. (2009). Panic disorder subtypes: deceptive somatic impersonators. *Psychiatry*, August, 6(8): 33–7. PMID: 19763206; PMCID: PMC2743212.
3 Ritter, M. (2018). Study: Neanderthals faced risks, but so did our ancestors. Phys.Org, November 14, phys.org/news/2018-11-neanderthals-ancestors.html
4 Kelly McCorry, L. (2007). Physiology of the autonomic nervous system. *American Journal of Pharmaceutic Education*, 15 August.
5 Arnsten, A. F. (2009). Stress signalling pathways that impair prefrontal cortex structure and function. *Nature Reviews Neuroscience*, 10(6): 410–22. https://doi.org/10.1038/nrn2648
6 Kolk, V. D., & Bessel, A. (2014). *The Body Keeps the Score: Brain, Mind, and Body in the Healing of Trauma*. Penguin.

Chapter 2

1 Herman, J. *The Body Keeps the Score: Brain, Mind, and Body in the Healing of Trauma* L. (2015). *Trauma and Recovery: The Aftermath of Violence—From Domestic Abuse to Political Terror*. Hachette UK.
2 Marksberry, K. (2022). *Holmes–Rahe Stress Inventory*. The American Institute of Stress. https://www.stress.org/holmes-rahe-stress-inventory
3 Understanding anxiety and depression for LGBTQ people (n.d.). Anxiety and Depression Association of America, ADAA. https://adaa.org/learn-from-us/from-the-experts/blog-posts/consumer/understanding-anxiety-and-depression-lgbtq#:~:text=Somewhere%20between%2030%20and%2060,straight%20or%20gender%2Dconforming%20counterparts
4 Fast facts: preventing adverse childhood experiences | Violence Prevention | InjuryCenter|CDC(n.d.).https://www.cdc.gov/violenceprevention/aces/fastfact.html
5 Aucoin, M., LaChance, L., Naidoo, U., Remy, D., Shekdar, T., Sayar, N., Cardozo, V., Rawana, T., Chan, I., & Cooley, K. (2021). Diet and anxiety: a scoping review. *Nutrients*, 13(12): 4418. https://doi.org/10.3390/nu13124418

Chapter 3

1 Edemekong, P. F. (2023). *Activities of Daily Living*. StatPearls - NCBI Bookshelf. https://www.ncbi.nlm.nih.gov/books/NBK470404/
2 https://www.sciencedirect.com/topics/immunology-and-microbiology/allostasis#:~:text=Allostasis%20is%20defined%20as%20the,meet%20perceived%20and%20anticipated%20demands
3 Billman, G. E. (2020). Homeostasis: the underappreciated and far too often ignored central organizing principle of physiology. *Frontiers in Physiology*, 11. https://doi.org/10.3389/fphys.2020.00200
4 Balaram, K. (2023). *Agoraphobia*. StatPearls – NCBI Bookshelf. https://www.ncbi.nlm.nih.gov/books/NBK554387/
5 Lane, P. (2023). *Understanding and Coping with Illness Anxiety*. Routledge.

Chapter 4

1 Brown, B. (2007). *I Thought It Was Just Me: Women Reclaiming Power and Courage in a Culture of Shame*. Gotham Books.
2 Hanh, T. N. (2002). *Anger: Wisdom for Cooling the Flames*. Penguin.

Chapter 5

1 *The Happiness Trap online program* (n.d.). The Happiness Trap. https://thehappinesstrap.com/
2 Hanh, T. N. (2015). *How to Walk*. National Geographic Books.

Chapter 6

1 Beck, A. T., Emery, G., & Greenberg, R. L. (1985). *Anxiety Disorders and Phobias*. Basic Books.
2 Beck, A. T. (1979). *Cognitive Therapy and the Emotional Disorders*. Penguin.
3 VandenBos, G. R. & APA (2015). *APA Dictionary of Psychology*. APA Books.
4 Linehan, M. M. (1993). *Skills Training Manual for Treating Borderline Personality Disorder*. http://ci.nii.ac.jp/ncid/BA20856529
5 Horney, K. (1950). *Neurosis and Human Growth: The Struggle toward Self-realization*. W. W. Norton & Company.

Chapter 7

1 Knafo, D. (2002). Revisiting Ernst Kris's concept of regression in the service of the ego in art. *Psychoanalytic Psychology*, 19(1): 24–49. https://doi.org/10.1037/0736-9735.19.1.24

2   Anxiety Educational Resources | Psychiatry | Michigan Medicine (2023). *Psychiatry*. https://medicine.umich.edu/dept/psychiatry/programs/anxiety-disorders-program-adult/anxiety-educational-resources

3   Umadevi, P., Ramachandra, Varambally, S., Philip, M., & Gangadhar, B. N. (2013). Effect of yoga therapy on anxiety and depressive symptoms and quality-of-life among caregivers of in-patients with neurological disorders at a tertiary care center in India: a randomized controlled trial. *Indian Journal of Psychiatry*. July, 55(Suppl 3): S385-9. doi: 10.4103/0019-5545.116304. PMID: 24049204; PMCID: PMC3768217.

4   Joaquín Selva, Bc.S. "What Is Self-Actualization? Meaning, Theory + Examples." *PositivePsychology.Com*, 4 Nov. 2024, positivepsychology.com/self-actualization/#:~:text=Physiological%20needs%20refer%20to%20things,esteem%20needs%20are%20already%20met.

5   Pacchierotti, C., Bossini, L., Castrogiovanni, A., Pieraccini, F., Soreca, I., & Castrogiovanni, P. (2002). Attachment and panic disorder. *Psychopathology*, 35(6), 347–54. https://doi.org/10.1159/000068597

6   Board, F.a.N. (2017). *Dietary Guidelines for Americans Guidelines and Key Recommendations*. Redesigning the Process for Establishing the Dietary Guidelines for Americans – NCBI Bookshelf. https://www.ncbi.nlm.nih.gov/books/NBK469839/#:~:text=5%20Overarching%20Guidelines&text=Focus%20on%20variety%2C%20nutrient%20density,healthy%20eating%20patterns%20for%20all

7   *Water* (2021). The Nutrition Source. https://www.hsph.harvard.edu/nutritionsource/water/

8   Office of the Commissioner (2023). *Spilling the Beans: How Much Caffeine Is Too Much?* U.S. Food and Drug Administration. https://www.fda.gov/consumers/consumer-updates/spilling-beans-how-much-caffeine-too-much#:~:text=For%20healthy%20adults%2C%20the%20FDA,it%20(break%20it%20down)

9   Current guidelines | Health.gov. (n.d.). https://health.gov/our-work/nutrition-physical-activity/physical-activity-guidelines/current-guidelines

10 Watson, N. F., Badr, M. S., Belenky, G., Bliwise, D. L., Buxton, O. M., Buysse, D., Dinges, D. F., Gangwisch, J., Grandner, M.A., Kushida, C., Malhotra, R. K., Martin J. L., Patel, S. R., Quan, S. F., & Tasali, E. (2015). Recommended amount of sleep for a healthy adult: a joint consensus statement of the American Academy of Sleep Medicine and Sleep Research Society. *Sleep*, June 1, 38(6): 843–4. doi: 10.5665/sleep.4716. PMID: 26039963; PMCID: PMC4434546.

Chapter 8

1   Bandura, A. (1997). *Self-Efficacy: The Exercise of Control*. Macmillan.
2   Poetry Foundation (1950). Auguries of Innocence by William Blake | Poetry Foundation. https://www.poetryfoundation.org/poems/43650/auguries-of-innocence
3   Yalom, I. D. (1980). *Existential Psychotherapy*. Basic Books.

Chapter 9

1   Freud, S. (1958) *Remembering, Repeating, and Working-Through (Further Recommendations on the Technique of Psycho-Analysis, II [1914])* in Standard Edition, vol. 12, trans. J. Strachey. Hogarth Press. 145–56.
2   Herman, J. L. (2015). *Trauma and Recovery: The Aftermath of Violence—From Domestic Abuse to Political Terror*. Hachette UK.

Index

Join the Sheldon Press community today, sign up for our newsletter!

- Select a **FREE eBook** or extract to read upon joining

- Keep up with our latest publishing and exciting author news

- Be the first to hear about book prize draws, free extracts, and upcoming author events

Simply scan the QR code below or head to www.sheldonpress.co.uk/newsletter to sign up.